Daughter of a Voice

I-Thou Encounters
in the Book of Genesis

Order this book online at www.trafford.com/07-1462
or email orders@trafford.com

Most Trafford titles are also available at major online book retailers.

Note for Librarians: A cataloguing record for this book is available from Library
and Archives Canada at www.collectionscanada.ca/amicus/index-e.html

Printed in Victoria, BC, Canada.

ISBN: 978-1-4251-3709-0

 www.trafford.com

North America & international
toll-free: 1 888 232 4444 (USA & Canada)
phone: 250 383 6864 ♦ fax: 250 383 6804 ♦ email: info@trafford.com

The United Kingdom & Europe
phone: +44 (0)1865 722 113 ♦ local rate: 0845 230 9601
facsimile: +44 (0)1865 722 868 ♦ email: info.uk@trafford.com

10 9 8 7 6 5 4 3 2

To See Your Face

Is

To See the Face of God

CONTENTS

PART C: AND THEIR WORDS TO THE END OF THE WORLD

APPENDIX

DEDICATION

To my Eternal Thou

To Bat Kol Staff, Board, alumni/ae

To my editor, poet and writer, Alexandra Leggat

To Ron Baker, existentialist and practitioner of Buber's I-Thou philosophy

To Angela Aidoo & Arthi Reddy at Trafford Publishing

To all whom I address as Thou

Thank YOU

INTRODUCTION

In the fall of 1972, while standing on the northern shore of Lake Superior, I had an unforgettable experience.

The time had come to move to Toronto. I had completed my studies and I had been offered a teaching position at the University. While I was delighted with the offer of a teaching position the thought of leaving my close friends wrenched my heart. Before making the final break with them, I had a brief respite, a previously planned two-week trip to the West of Canada. On the return trip as I drove mile after mile through large areas of wilderness in Northern Ontario and along the shoreline of Lake Superior, the pain of having to separate increased. At a juncture in the road, on the northeastern tip of Lake Superior, I stopped to rest. When I got out of the car I saw below me the expanse of the largest fresh water lake in the world.

The lake was still. Not a ripple on the surface. Scraggly pine trees that dotted the area had the battle look of years of struggle with strong winds that whipped across the lake. Hundreds of seagulls flew low, plaintively crying. The stark isolation and loneliness of the scene described my soul.

As I stood there, a lonely isolated individual, something happened to me. Before I knew it, the walls that separated me from the world crumbled. The boundaries of my isolated self melted into a friendly relationship with nature. I was no longer apart from the world but one with it. The lake in its glistening beauty rose up to greet me. The various shades of green in the trees and grasses enveloped me in their beautiful textured robes. The slow flying seagulls floated closer with words of comfort. Though Ottawa was still hundreds of miles away, distance had disappeared. A profound peace, a most welcome guest, had entered my soul.

Reflecting on this later, I found words to describe the experience. I had had an I/Thou encounter.

Martin Buber, the Jewish philosopher of dialogue, best known for his book, *I and Thou*, describes our relationship to reality, not only with people, but with animals and plants and even rocks, by the use of two paired words, I-Thou and I-It.[1] He describes an I-Thou relationship as a relationship of dialogue where the other is received unconditionally without judgment and without expectations. An I-It relationship is a relationship of an I to an Object, where the object can be studied, described and used. Both kinds of relationships are valid and necessary but a world of *only* I-It relationships is numbing, while relationships of I-Thou are life giving. At any moment an I-It relationship can pass into an I-Thou encounter and vice versa, an I-Thou encounter can suddenly become an I-It relationship.

The Book of Genesis, a book of interesting personalities, portrays various shades and forms of I-Thou and I-It encounters. In the opening chapters of Genesis, you will learn that God created the universe in order to have a dialogue partner, actually several dialogue partners, because God speaks not only to humans but to plants and rocks and animals, as well. By the time you reach the last chapter, you will learn that events, yes, ordinary everyday events, speak and present themselves to you to be encountered and responded to.

A life of dialogue! A life of encounter! The art of living is learning how to be in relationship. Meditation on the biblical characters in the book of Genesis provides lessons on how to live in relationship with the world, with humanity, with God.

Because I want this book to help you to enter into I-Thou relationships I will try to keep it friendly. By that I mean that I will not fill it with quotations or authors' names, though I will be using the wisdom of the sages. Nor will I insert multiple biblical references into the flow of the text. Each of the chapters in this book will follow the recognized divisions of the Hebrew bible, which will be noted at the beginning of the chapter as well as in the table of contents. As a literary device I will put words into the mouths of the biblical characters, even of angels and demons but you should not get distracted by whether or not demons and angels exist, but focus rather on what they say. The sages have often used this device in the past and it is known as Midrash.

Finally, since I believe that there is no impression without expression, I have included exercises for reflection at the end of each chapter. You may use these for personal journal writing, with a bible study group or with another person. Above all, use this book in a manner that gives you joy and life.

---

1   Buber, Martin, *I and Thou*, trans.,W. Kaufmann, (New York, 1970).

PART A

DAY TO DAY POURS FORTH SPEECH

The Creation of Light. *Gustave Dore*

1A.

Encountering the Eternal Thou

God's presence in each element[2]

> **Genesis**
> *Bereshit*
> 1:1 –6:8

KIVYAKHOL! AS IT Were! An exuberant world came slowly and steadily into existence as God pronounced ten words composed of letters from the divine Name, beginning with, *Yehi*, "Let it be." God looked out on this world and said, "Very good, very good, indeed!"

What was so good? The Word had become incarnate in various manifestations, colors and forms. Paths were strewn with light, flowers thrilled into bloom, trees nodded to each other, the wild animals moved slowly, the stars whirled in dances of complex rhythms, and multi-toned music echoed from innumerable worlds.

"Now what?" God said to the divine self! That was a rhetorical question for God knew what God would do. God said, "I will make an earthling, Adam, like unto myself. I will make the earthling of *adama*, earth. I will place within its being a portion of myself, a divine spark, so that we can knowingly communicate with each other."

Once God had made that decision, God announced it to the heavenly hosts. When they heard it, they, with the Seraphim[3] leading, broke out in chorus, "Holy, Holy, Holy, Yah, God of hosts, describe your plan to us again." God told them of the divine intention to create a human being who would have a dual personality. "Each earthling will be both human and divine, mortal and immor-

---

2 All quotations in the chapter headings are from Martin Buber's classic *I and Thou*.
3 Isaiah 6

tal, and will possess an ability to talk with humans and with angels. Moreover, because each will possess a divine spark it will forever be drawn towards me and I will always know where the earthling is because of our connection."

The heavenly hosts responded with a heavenly buzz of sounds like cymbals, rustling of wings, wind and running waters. The Ofanim[4] spoke up, "Blessed are You, *Ein Sof*, the Endless One, the boundless One, nameless and faceless. You are everywhere. Where will room exist for such a creature because you fill all places? And how will it address you as Thou?"

"That is a good question," God said. "The answer is *tsimtsum*—divine self-limitation out of love. I will withdraw some of my presence so that the earthling has room to exist, room to make decisions, and room to be free to say *Yes* to me and *No* to me.

Now, winged fiery beings known as Seraphim stood above the throne of God chanting, "Blessed be your holy name, *Elohim, Hagadol, Hagibor, Hanorah*—God, the Great, the Powerful, the Awesome," stopped their song, bowed gracefully and asked, "You are a God of Justice. When this earthling disobeys you, You, Elohim, will have to destroy the rebellious creature. Why create a being that might have to be destroyed?"

Taken aback, God said, "Ah, you know me as *Elohim*, God of Justice. And so I am. But as you say, something is lacking. I need to find an answer to the problem you raised."

God turned away from the Seraphim, withdrew into the divine self for some moments, and then, from deep within, God drew forth the attribute of Mercy. Turning back to the Seraphim, God said, "Here is Mercy, packaged in my new name, YHWH (LORD)." The Seraphim were stunned for the Name glowed and sent out warm currents of comfort. "YAH..., YAH..., YAH...," they chanted. They could see how those letters needed to be pronounced but they couldn't get the full sound out. Finally, one of the sharpest of the Seraphim cried out, *Halleluyah*, meaning "praise YAH." Then all the Seraphim sang, "HalleluYAH, HalleluYAH, HalleluYAH." From behind a column, one of the smallest of the Seraphim came forward, "Yah," it pleaded. "How will this name of mercy prevent an earthling from being destroyed." God smiled at the little seraph and said, "I will do two plantations of my name YHWH in the heart of each earthling. When the earthling sins, one of my Names will leave but the other Name will call out longingly

---

4   Ezekiel 1. 15-21

to the departed Name. The sinner will feel discomfort and remorse at this tug of war and will repent. When the sinner repents, and Repentance is another gift I will bestow upon the earthling, the two Names will be reunited and the sinner will feel at home with me again."

At that moment, the Cherubim[5], mobile winged beings with voices like the sound of many winds, called out: "Blessed be your holy name, *Ha-Makom*, The Place."

Not to be outdone in name calling, the *Hayyot* came forward on a cloud of great brightness with fire flashing forth. In the middle of the fire was something like gleaming amber and in the midst of the amber four living creatures, the *Hayyot*, each with four faces and four wings[6]. They said, "Blessed be your holy name, *Ha-Rahaman* (the All Merciful One). Please further enlighten us. You talk about *tsimtsum*, divine self-limitation. If you withdraw yourself from the world, how will the world exist?

And God said, "You must understand *tsimtsum*, the limitation of myself through love. It's like I have two hands. One of my hands is my immortal, unchanging, unmoved Self. My other hand that I am about to reveal is my ever-flowing Life Force that will be the life of all living things. My relationship to the world will not be in the manner of two separate entities Creator and creature but rather as deep structure and surface. Scratch the surface of reality and I can be discovered. The path to me will be more like peeling off the layers of an onion than climbing a ladder to the sky. The Earthling will be able to discover me anywhere when the earthling addresses me as Thou. The place I am about to create will be called *Olam*. World, *Olam (hidden)*, is the place where I will be hidden and can be found in both joy and sorrow. Like a woman in labor I too can gasp and pant."

Three angels came forward: Raphael, Michael, Gabriel: "Oh, Holy One, we know that you will be sending us to earth as your messengers. Please tell us by what standard these earthlings, these humans, are to live."

God was particularly pleased with that question. God said, "I will give them my *Torah*, my Word."

Raphael whose name means *God heals*, said: "The Torah of the LORD is perfect, reviving the soul; the decrees of the LORD are sure, making wise the simple."

---

5   Psalm 18.10; Psalm 99.1
6   Isaiah 6

Michael whose name means *Who is like God*, said: "The precepts of the LORD are right, rejoicing the heart; the commandment of the LORD is clear, enlightening the eyes."

Gabriel whose name means *God is my strength*, said: "The fear of the LORD is pure, enduring forever; the ordinances of the LORD are true and righteous altogether."

At that, the whole heavenly court joined in chorus:

> More to be desired are they than gold,
>   even much fine gold;
> sweeter also than honey,
>   and drippings of the honeycomb.[7]

God dismissed the heavenly court and disappeared from sight. On the seventh day when God was resting in honor of creation, the heavenly hosts gathered around wanting to know what God had done. God drew back a veil to let them see. Spontaneously and all together, they broke into song:

> Holy, holy, holy is the LORD of hosts;
> the whole earth is full of your glory.[8]

Slowly and deliberately, God withdrew another veil. There stood Adam and Eve in all their majesty and glory. The heavenly hosts cried out: " Marvelous! Incredible!"

> O Holy One, you have made them but little lower than the angels.
> You have crowned them with glory and honor.
> Oh, YAH, our God!
> How glorious is your name in all the earth."[9]

There is no Impression without Expression

1.Encounters fall roughly into three categories: encounters that are accidental, encounters with an agenda in mind, and encounters simply to be

---

7   Psalm 19: 7-10
8   Isaiah 6.3
9   Psalm 8

together. Obviously an I-Thou encounter would fall into the last category where there is no agenda. That being so, it is possible for you to have an authentic I-Thou encounter not only with another person but also with a stone, a tree or an animal. Some of these encounters will obviously be accidental because accidental encounters have no agenda.

If you apply these categories to your encounter with a tree you can begin to see the difference. If you approach a tree, address it and expect an answer from the tree you will be disappointed because you have an agenda. But if you approach the tree realizing that it was there before you and has already addressed you as a Thou, you may be moved to respond. Your response may be one of awe as you behold its leafy arms outstretched to you.

According to Buber the living wholeness and unity of a tree denies itself to the eye of anyone who merely investigates it. The potential of plants and animals for a mutual relationship of I-Thou is latent and is only awakened when an "I" approaches the plant or animal as a Thou. The threshold of mutuality for animals and plants differs. Animals can be tamed. They can learn to respond tenderly to human initiatives. Yet, a plant, though not capable of this level of mutuality, will also respond if you approach it as an I to a Thou.

Think of your own encounter with a sunset and its effect on you.

2. Time is an important element in authentic encounter. The artist Georgia O'Keefe wrote, "To see takes time." Theodore Roethke[10] believes that if you look at a thing long enough, you will become part of it and it will become a part of you. You will break away from self-involvement, from I to Otherwise, or maybe even to the eternal Thou.

Think of a pleasant moment you have had during the past month or year. Stay with it. Before you turn from the memory, feel the power of rejuvenation in the memory.

3. Long before the first chapter of John's Gospel was written, the Word had become flesh. When God said, "Let it be!" and "it was," God's Word became embodied. Arthur Green,[11] the Jewish mystic, wrote, "Our religion indeed may be called incarnational. God is *ruah kol basar*, the spirit resides in all flesh."

The Word made flesh! Recall an encounter with the Word?

---

10   Reed, Madness, The Price of Poetry, see Roethke (London, 1989).
11   Green, A. *Seek My Face*. (Vermont, 2003)

Creation of Adam and Eve. *Gustave Dore*

1B.

I AND THOU

Presence becomes real in the reality of the hallowed life of the world

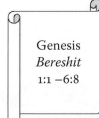

Genesis
Bereshit
1:1 −6:8

KIVYAKHOL! AS IT Were! The three archangels Michael, Raphael and Gabriel stood in amazement before Adam and Eve. They did not allow themselves to be seen or heard. Michael[12], a handsome prince clothed in garments white as snow, said to Raphael and Gabriel, "You know that my name means, *Who is like El* (God)! Yet, see these godlike humans."

Then Michael picked up the Torah and read:
Let us make humankind in our image, according to our likeness...So God created humankind in his image, in the image of God he created them.

Putting the book down, Michael said, "There can be no doubt about it. Three times it is written, 'made in the image of God.' Every human possesses a portion of the divine self! Are we now to bow to this earthling!"

Gabriel,[13] the elegant messenger, known as the left hand of God and whose name means, *Strong with God*, said to Michael, "It says in the Torah, 'God created the earthling in the divine image, in the image of God, God created *it*; male and female created God *them*.'[14] *It* became *them*, *one* became *two*. A division! *Ish*, man, and *Isha*, woman. Related yet different. And see, look, there is God's name, *Yah*, buried in the combination of the Hebrew letters

---

12 Book of Daniel and the Book of Revelation (12.7).
13 Daniel 8. 15-17; Luke 1.
14 Gen. 1.27. Note the change from the singular to the plural in the Hebrew text.

of *Ish* and *Isha*. A portion of God is in them. Perhaps we do need to bow down to them!"

Unannounced and unexpected, the Accuser, HaSatan, in star-studded trailing black robes burst on to the scene. He stood erect and rather disdainfully looked at Michael and Gabriel. Turning to Raphael, the healing archangel, he said, "You will need all your healing powers. These two are not just divine beings with an inclination, the *yetzer hatov*, towards good, but earthlings with an inclination, the *yetzer harah*, towards excess. I'm related to the *yetzer harah*, and I will succeed in leading them down shady and dangerous paths. You will shortly know of my power!"

Suddenly all became silent in heaven and the heavenly hosts looked to earth and saw something they had never seen before. Adam *knew* his wife Eve. She conceived and bore a son, Cain. When she saw the little creature that emerged from her, she cried out, "I have produced a child with the help of the Lord." Next she bore his brother Abel.

The archangels Michael, Gabriel and Raphael stood in wonder. This couple is like God. Like God, they too can create!

Adam and Eve quickly learned that life wasn't just a bed of roses. Adam said to Eve, "Is there a battle going on inside you? I feel I have two ropes around my neck, one rope tying me to heaven and the other to earth. Sometimes I feel a jerk from the rope above and at other times from the rope below."

Eve answered, "I do, too. Those ropes are our two inclinations, the *yetzer hatov* and the *yetzer harah*. When they both start pulling in different directions, I don't know which one I should obey."

"Yes, you do," Adam countered, "we learned that lesson when we ate the fruit of the tree that God told us not to eat. I wonder what my life would be like if I hadn't listened to you."

"You know what, Adam! God prefers someone who stands up to the divine Self. Yes, I took my stand against God and we're paying the penalty. But God didn't stop loving us. I don't think God likes yes-men!"

"You're right, Eve. But we have been given the Torah. The words of Torah are life."

"Yes, Adam, But don't forget those other words, *Na'aseh vey nishmah* (we will do and we will hear). We also learn from our mistakes. How else would we have learned the lesson of *midat hadin*, measure for measure! We reap the fruits of our actions."

Life taught Adam and Eve many lessons. After a particularly exciting day in the field, Adam said to Eve, "I sowed wheat seeds in the ground and wheat plants came up. I sowed mustard seeds and mustard seedlings sprouted."

Eve smiled, "We thought we lost God when we were expelled from the Garden but I think God is mysteriously present everywhere and talks to us in all these things. Your seeds, for example, tell us once again that what we sow, we reap. *Midat hadin!* Did you see that mustard plant of yours? It is now a tree and the birds of the air are nesting in it. Such a small seed and such a great tree. When I was making bread yesterday, I put a bit of yeast into the dough and I made several loaves from the same batch instead of one pita bread. Such good results from such a small deed. Do you think that we could be like yeast in the world and create a world like we had in the Garden of Eden?"

Adam responded after a moment's thought, "Eve, that is called *tikkun olam*, mending the world."

Adam and Eve learned to address each other as their other self. They liked to call each other by name. They knew the meaning of their names. Adam from *adamah*, earth, and Eve, Mother of the Living. One day Adam said to Eve, "Do you remember when I called you, Eve? I saw you before you saw me. I remember my astonishment. I cried out, 'flesh of my flesh, blood of my blood.' You were so beautiful!" Eve winced. When Adam saw that Eve heard him speaking in the past tense, he quickly added, "Oh, but you are even more beautiful today after 800 years."

Eve took a step towards him, "Let me hug you, Adam." Holding out her hands in a broad sweep, she added, "Remember that God created us with the divine hands and not just with the divine word, 'Let it be.' And not just suddenly and mechanically! God molded us and fondled us as God shaped us. God kissed us, too, as God blew the divine breath into our nostrils. God will continue to create. A new creation is revelation." Adam didn't know where Eve got this information but he opened his arms to receive her embrace. The chipmunks and squirrels laughed and giggled. In fact, the whole world, all the plants and the animals began to smile.

Time passed. One day, Eve said to Adam, in solemn tones, "Do you remember the birth of our first son, Cain? When I saw this baby boy in my arms, I was outside myself with joy and I cried out, look at what God has given to me! And I held him up to you. He grew quickly. Remember how he liked to till the land with you. He was a real farmer at heart. After his birth though I wanted a little girl. So did you. But God gave us Abel instead. He was as marvelous as his brother and we both soon forgot that we wanted a baby girl. But our second son didn't like farming. He became a shepherd instead."

Adam told Eve that he didn't want to talk anymore about that. Adam was afraid to make Eve sad again. Cain had killed his brother Abel in an act of envy. It was the first murder that had ever occurred in the world. They were so shocked at the sight of the earth soaking up the blood of Abel, that even today, years later, the scene came before them as though it were yesterday.

Eve looked tearfully at Adam and she said, "I know you don't want to upset me. But we must talk about it. We must never forget our failings, Adam, for from them we can learn."

Adam drew closer to Eve and said, "You remember how God talked to our son. He saw that Cain was jealous and he told him not to envy his brother but only to look at his own deeds and be happy with what he could do. But our son couldn't get his envy of Abel out of his heart and so he killed him."

Eve pressed Adam's hand and said, "Yes, though Cain killed his brother, God had a long conversation with him. God still loved him. Though he would be a wanderer on the earth, God would protect his life."

They both sat silently knowing what the other was thinking. Cain not only killed Abel but he extinguished something of God's presence from the earth. They learned that the blood of every human being that is spilled on the earth cries to God to be heard.

Eve sighed, "I hope our children will learn from their mistakes as we have learned from ours."

"They will if they but cling to the Torah," replied Adam. "God told us, 'My Word is a lamp for your feet.'"

After Abel's death, Seth was born. Then they had more children and their children had children and these children had children and the world became populated. Adam and Eve lived a very long time. Then they died. In the book of genealogy it was written:

This is the list of the descendants of Adam. When God created humankind, he made them in the likeness of God. Male and female he created them, and he blessed them and named them "Humankind" when they were created.

There is no Impression without Expression

1. The following people have found metaphors to describe their encounter with God:

> *Theresa of Avila, a Spanish mystic of the sixteenth century, described the soul of every new born child as a most beautiful crystal globe, made in the shape of a castle, and containing seven mansions, in the seventh and innermost of which is God, in the greatest splendor, illuminating and beautifying them all. At this level the soul and God are conjoined in the manner, so to speak, of two lighted candles which have joined and become one or as the falling rain becomes merged in the river.*[15]

> *Karl Rahner, a modern German theologian of the nineteenth century, wrote that a purely natural person does not exist, that when a child is born into the world it comes into this world a natural/supernatural creature having been raised to the supernatural level through the gift of grace. The presence of God and the human person are so intermingled that in "one way or other both remain indestructible and interdependent...(although) the very obscurity of the presence of each in the other means that they can appear to be separated".*[16]

---

15   Teresa of Avila, The *Interior Castle* (New York, 1989*).*
16   Karl Rahner quoted in, *Revelation and Self-Understanding*, M. Fritz, Ph.D. thesis, Ottawa, Canada, 1991, p. 49.

> *Rabbi Dov Baer of Lubavich (1773-1827)[17] and the Sefat Emet[18] taught*
> *that the innermost center of the soul is the yechida, a divine point*
> *that is permanently attached to God for it is an actual portion of*
> *God's own Self. This divine point, the nekudah, is infinite smallness*
> *that is infinite vastness, a limitless oneness that contains the entire*
> *world within in for it is bound and at one with its Source.*

What metaphor would you use to describe your relationship with God?

2. God is above and below and around and within. God dwells in the world of *relation*. Buber writes that relationships can be built in three different spheres, life with nature, life with humans and life with spiritual beings: "In every sphere, in every relational act, through everything that becomes present to us, we gaze toward the train of the eternal Thou; in each we perceive a breath of it; in every Thou we address the eternal Thou, in every sphere according to its manner."[19]

Think of your last twenty-four hours, or forty-eight hours. In any of those hours are you aware that you caught a glimpse of the train of the eternal Thou? Did you perceive a breath of the divine? Perhaps you even addressed the eternal Thou in a person, a place or a book?

3. Though God's mysterious presence is everywhere our experience of the I-Thou is not always one of light. On the contrary, the bible is full of examples of an I-Thou experience of darkness (Genesis 15.12; 32:24; Exodus 4:24-26; Luke 22.42-44). Buber wrote, "We know from the life of the founders of religions...that there is such an 'event of the night'; the sudden collapse of the newly-won certainty, the 'deadly factual' moment when the demon working with apparently unbounded authority appears in the world where God alone had been in control but a moment before."

Look back on one of your "nights of the Lord." You couldn't sleep. You were worried. You felt trapped. Recall that a trap has two doors. Did you go out the front door or the back door? What was waiting for you there?

4. The groom, God, in the *Song of Songs*, addresses you in these words,

---

17 Louis Jacob, trans. and annotator, On *Ecstasy: A Tract by Dobh Baer* (New York. 1963); Louis Jacobs, *Jewish Mystical Testimonies* (New York. 1976).
18 See, Arthur Green, *The Language of Truth: The Torah Commentary of the Sefat Emet* (Philadelphia, 1998).
19 Buber, *I and Thou* (New York, 1970).

I AND THOU

My dove in the clefts of the rock,
In the shadow of the cliff,
Let me see you, all of you!
Let me hear your voice,
Your delicious song.
I love to look at you.

How do you respond to this address? Is your response in the form of a word or an action?

Replace With

With

COLOUR

INSERT

Replace With COLOUR INSERT

Rainbow-sign of tl

2.

AN INCAPACITY TO RELATE

The presence of the Thou moves over the world of It
Like the spirit upon the face of the waters.

Genesis
Noah
6:9 – 11:32

WHEN LAMECH, A distant descendant of Adam and Eve, had lived one hundred eighty-two years, he became the father of a son; he named him Noah, saying, "This one shall bring us relief from our work and from the toil of our hands."

The young Noah grew up in an evil environment. The inhabitants of the world no longer listened to God nor did they study Torah. As Noah grew older he withdrew from the world for as he said to himself, "These people only listen to their *yetzer harah*, their evil inclination and pay no attention to their *yetzer hatov*, their good inclination." Noah didn't know it but his own *yetzer hatov* was dulled by the evil in the world. He had lost his sensitivity to the sufferings around him. His ability and willingness to relate to his neighbors were near zero tolerance. Despite this he was known as the Righteous One in his generation because he didn't participate in their idol worship, the abuse of children and women and other evil practices that had spread like weeds and filled the atmosphere with a fowl smelling spirit. Had he lived in a generation where the inhabitants feared and loved God he would not have been considered outstanding for he was basically unconcerned about others.

God grieved because of the corruption that had spread to the ends of the earth. God said to the divine Self, "I will not hide from Noah what I am about to do. What I tell Noah may awake him from his apathy and shake him into action." When God appeared to Noah, Noah was five hundred years old. He had a wife, Naamah[20], and three sons, Shem, Ham, and Japheth.[21] While Noah was having lunch with them one day, not talking, as was his custom, he felt a strong urge to go out into the field. He got up and walked out. When he had gone but a mere hundred meters he heard a voice that said, "Noah, I have determined to make an end of all flesh, for the earth is filled with violence; now I am going to destroy all living things along with the earth. I am going to bring a flood of waters on the earth, to destroy from under heaven all flesh in which is the breath of life; everything that is on the earth shall die. But I will establish my covenant with you; and you shall come into the ark, you, your sons, your wife, and your sons' wives. And of every living thing, of all flesh, you shall bring two of every kind, male and female, into the ark, to keep them alive with you."

Noah nodded YES to God.[22] He didn't speak. He didn't even seem to be shocked. He walked back to the house and continued eating his meal with Naamah and his three sons, as though nothing had happened.

Noah had a guardian angel whose name was Ariel, meaning *Lion of God*, who cared about the earth and all its inhabitants. Time for Ariel didn't exist. All time was present, though when Ariel spoke to Noah Ariel talked the language that Noah understood. One day Ariel drew close to Noah and whispered to him, "Noah, be like Moses, one of your descendants. When God told him that the people were going to be destroyed and he alone would live and become a great nation, Moses argued with God. Moses said to God, 'O YHWH (YAH), why does your wrath burn hot against your people? Turn from your fierce wrath; change your mind and do not bring disaster on your people.' God listened to Moses. God decided not to destroy the people and did not bring about the planned disaster. Do the same, Noah. Argue with God. Tell God that you will help the people to do *teshuvah* (repentance)." Noah heard what Ariel said but Ariel's words were like buzzing flies in Noah's brain. He lifted his arm to swat them.

The next day, Noah went out and planted cypress seeds. He saw the seeds sprout and grow into tall trees with erect close branches. He often walked among the trees to measure their growth. He did not notice their fragrant smell nor sniff the strong aroma they gave off in the evening. From time to time, a neighbor would ask him what he was doing but Noah did not an-

---

20   Midrash Genesis Rabbah 23:4
21   Genesis 5
22   Genesis 6.22

swer. After a hundred years, when the trees were fully grown he cut them down, made the reddish colored wood into slats and built the ark according to God's instructions.

When the ark was built, God came to Noah a second time and said to him; "Go into the ark, you and all your household, for I have seen that you alone are righteous before me in this generation. For in seven days I will send rain on the earth for forty days and forty nights; and every living thing that I have made I will blot out from the face of the ground."

The angel tapped Noah again on the shoulder. "Argue with God. Stop God from doing this." But Noah did it, according to all that YHWH had commanded him.[23]

In the six hundredth year of Noah's life all the wellsprings of the great Ocean and the sluices of the heavens opened up. On that very day, Noah with his sons Shem, Ham and Japheth, and his wife, Naamah, and the three wives of his sons rushed into the ark, he and all living things designated by God, "as God had commanded him."[24]

Then YHWH closed the door and shut them in.

The rain fell and flowed in ever widening streams of swirling, rushing, violent waters that destroyed all in its path. Above the treetops and the mountains, the waters rose. All flesh died. Every living thing that had in it the breath of life, died. Every living thing on the face of the ground and birds of the air—all died.

At the end of forty days the rain stopped, the waters subsided and the ark came to rest upon the mountains of Ararat. Noah opened the window of the Ark and sent out a raven. The raven flew off but returned for the waters had not yet dried up from upon the earth. Then he sent out a dove but the dove returned, for the earth was still not dry. He waited seven days and sent the dove out a second time. The dove returned with a freshly plucked olive leaf and Noah" knew that the waters had subsided from upon the earth."[25]

Ariel tapped him again on his shoulder, "Noah, go out. It's time to leave."

---

23 Genesis 7.5
24 Genesis 7. 11-16
25 Genesis 8.11

But Noah waited.[26] He sent out the dove again. The dove did not return.

Ariel wrapped its wing over its eyes and said, "What is wrong with this man! Why doesn't he leave? Is he waiting for God to tell him to move? Can't he sense any of God's desires?"

When God saw that he did not leave, God said, "Go out of the Ark, you, your wife, your family and all living things, that you may all multiply and bear fruit." So Noah went out.[27]

Noah wasn't the same man coming out of the ark that he was going in. While in the Ark he came to himself and said, "I'm responsible for this flood. I never showed any feeling of sadness that an entire generation was to be lost, that the world was to be destroyed, that people had lost their way and surrendered to their *yetzer harah*. I never challenged God. I never expressed any words of concern, of solicitude or sadness. I felt no tenderness, no feelings of regret that these people though they were wicked would be lost. I was like a dead man walking. I didn't leap forward and beg God for them. I didn't tell God that I would arrange meetings with different individuals and groups. Alas, I see now, that I am guilty, that the flood waters will be called after me."[28]

When Noah came out of the ark, he built an altar to God and offered sacrifice on it. God was pleased. God was so touched by Noah's repentance that God decided to repent also. After all, God said to the divine Self, "I'm also to blame. I was the one who created the human with the *yetzer harah*. The inclination of the human heart is evil from youth; I will never again destroy every living creature as I have done."[29]

Grieved over the destruction of the original creation, God addressed the whole family of Noah and Naamah. God said, in solemn tender tones, "I am establishing my covenant with you and your descendants after you, and with every living creature that is with you. I have set my bow in the clouds,

---

26 *Genesis Midrash Rabbah*, XXXIV 4: Noah argued: Just as I entered the ark only when I was permitted, so may I not go out save with permission. R. Judah b. R. Ilai said: Had I been there I would have broken it and gone out! Noah, however, said: I entered with permission and I will leave with permission. Thus (the words): "Come thou into the ark;" "And Noah went in;" "Go forth from the ark; "and Noah went forth."

27 Genesis 8. 1-19.

28 Isaiah 54.9. "For when God bade Noah save himself and his household in the ark from the universal destruction at the time of the Flood, he did not intercede on behalf of his generation, but let them perish. It is for this reason that the waters of the Flood are named after him, as it is written, "for this is as the waters of Noah unto me." (*The Torah: A Modern Commentary*, ed., G. Plaut. New York, 1981).

29 Genesis 8.21

and it shall be a sign of the covenant between me and the earth. When I see the bow and when you see the bow we will all remember that I have made this covenant with you and all living things." After extending a blessing to the family and all living things, God added, "Listen carefully now to what I have to say. And don't forget these words I am about to pronounce." God paused. The family waited in suspense. Then God said, "Whoever sheds the blood of any human shall be accountable to me for the blood shed, for in my own image have I made each human person."

At that God disappeared from sight. Noah looked at his family tenderly yet said nothing. He went out into the field and he saw that the grapes on his vines were ripe. He made wine from them, drank it and became drunk. His son Ham found him lying naked in his tent. He was so disgusted that he castrated him, forgetting what God had just said to them about shedding the blood of a human being.[30] When Noah awoke from his stupor, he saw what his son had done. The shock to his system was so great that it loosened his tongue and he began to speak. He cursed the perpetrators of evil and blessed those who did good.

Naamah came to her husband Noah in great sorrow for the tragedy that had just happened to the two of them. It meant that they would have no more children. But she did her best to comfort him. He too could now speak so they had moments of intimacy unlike any that they had before. Their children and their grandchildren loved to see Noah and Naamah together. They thought they spent so much time together to make up for all the years Noah couldn't speak. But they were growing old. Noah was now nine hundred years old. He had been five hundred years old when the flood began. So they both lived a long time together.

There is no Impression without Expression

1. Abraham goes out the front door of the tent when he tries to save the people of Sodom. Jonah goes out the back door when he runs to Joppa. Which door does Noah go out? What was Noah's responsibility to God, to his society, to his family? Later, Noah's son treated him like an object. Did he learn that from Noah?

2. Do your animals go hungry? Are there hungry people in your town? Are there lonely people in your town? Do you feel fragmented by these ques-

---

30 Plaut, *The Torah: A Modern Commentary*, op. cit., p. 70.

tions? If so, thank God. Only fragmented people move.

3. Relationships are formed through the simple act of listening to another. Yet how often when another is speaking are we busy thinking of our response. True listening is a form of emptying one's mind in order to be truly present to the other person. And then having heard, respond.

Why didn't Noah hear the pain in God's voice? What were you thinking about the last time someone was trying to have a conversation with you?

4. Listening is directly proportionate to interest and care. What did God say that Noah didn't hear or didn't want to hear?

5. Did Noah really want the people to hear the Word of God? Are there times when you don't want people to hear the word of God? Do you want them to make a mistake?

The Call of Abraham. *Gustave Dore*

3.

The Voice of Dissatisfaction

Whoever goes forth in truth to meet the world goes forth to God

RAIN FELL SOFTLY on Abram's head and that of his brothers Nahor and Haran as they left the temple with their father, Terah. Abram was in a quiet mood as his brothers and father talked about Nanna, the God of the moon. Terah reminded them that Nanna is a Sumerian name that means "illuminator" and that in Haran he is known as Sin, the "father of the gods". Sin had a beard made of lapis lazuli and he rode on a winged bull. He had two chief seats of worship, Ur, where the family was living and Haran, where Terah decided he would move with his family. Nomadic peoples believed the moon-god guided and protected them at night. The more Abram thought about the moon-god the more uncomfortable he became.

> Genesis
> *Lekh Lekha*
> 12:1 – 17:27

Abraham and Sarah hear God's Voice

Abram sold images in his father's shop. He became more and more dissatisfied with his work because he knew his customers invested these images with power and bowed down to them. He roamed about in his mind asking questions that seemed to have no answers. How long shall we bow down to the work of our own hands? It is not right to worship and bow down to anything but the earth, which brings forth fruit and sustains us. When he saw that the earth needs rain, and that without the sky opening and sending down rain, the earth would grow nothing at all, he thought, it is not right to bow down to anything but the sky. When he looked up and saw the sun that gives light to the world and brings forth the plants, he thought, it is not right to bow down to anything but the sun. When he saw the sun setting, he thought, that is no god. He looked again at the moon and the stars that give light at night, and thought, to these it is right to bow down. But when the dawn broke, they were all effaced, and he thought, these are no gods.

Abram was greatly distressed by all these endless questions that seemed to have no answers. He often talked to Sarai about them. He found comfort in Sarai for she too had the same questions. They both felt a great dissatisfaction with the lives they were living. Abram had thought that Sarai would satisfy his restless heart and Sarai felt that Abram would be the answer to her deep longings. Not only were they husband and wife, they were like brother and sister. Though they had moments of great intimacy where the boundaries that separated them into separate lonely lives disappeared, these moments were fleeting.

Then one day Abram returned later than usual from work. When he entered the house Sarai saw that he was greatly agitated. "What happened, Abram, what is wrong with you?" Abram looked into Sarai's eyes and said, "I was alone in the shop today when a man came in to buy statues. He wanted thirty of them to pass around to his friends. I was so upset, I took a club and said, you think these are your gods! This is what I think of your gods! And with that I picked up a club and smashed them all, right there in front of him. The man was so shocked he fled from the shop screaming. When my father entered and saw all the images smashed except for one in the corner, he angrily asked, what has happened here? I was terrified and pointing to the opposite corner, I said, that god there got angry with all the others and smashed them.

Sarai grasped his shaking hand. "Abram," she said, "we have to leave here and quickly. I can no longer stand it here. I'm barren. The whole atmosphere is barren. Nothing but death exists here for us." And she began to sob. When Abram looked at the tears rolling down the cheeks of his beautiful wife, he was deeply shaken within himself. He couldn't sleep that night. When he saw that his wife was in a deep sleep he slipped out into the night. He looked up into the sky and saw a half crescent moon. "That surely can't be God," he thought, "beautiful as it is."

Now God had provoked the dissatisfaction in both their hearts. A strange cure exists for barrenness (*akarah*) and that cure is more barrenness (*ak-*

rut).[31] God's plans for them demanded attentive hearing, a type of hearing that could not be heard in satisfaction, so God kept raising the level of discomfort in both of them. Neither of them evaded the questions God raised in their minds. Sometimes the questions posed by their situation seemed intolerable. When God saw they were ready for the command, God said to Abram:

> *Lekh Lekha*! Go from your country and your kindred and your father's house to the land that I will show you. I will make of you a great nation, and I will bless you, and make your name great, so that you will be a blessing. I will bless those who bless you, and the one who curses you I will curse; and in you all the families of the earth shall be blessed."[32]

When Abram returned to the house, Sarai saw that he looked different. A deep peace radiated from his eyes. She knew he had discovered something or someone. "What happened?" she asked. "I heard a Voice," replied Abram. "I'm not sure whose Voice but it was real and I feel the truth of it. We have to leave here, now." When he told Sarai what he had heard, she asked him, "Did the Voice tell you where we are to go?" "No," replied Abram, but the Voice said, 'I will show you the way.'" Sarai sensed in the pit of her stomach that they would be on the way for a long time, wandering here and there until they found the place.[33] But she was ready to go.

Physical Wandering and Mental Wandering

Within hours they left. Abram, now seventy-five years old and Sarai, sixty-six, left with Lot, the son of Abram's brother, Haran, and all their possessions. By the end of the first day of traveling, Abram and Sarai breathed more freely. The air felt lighter. Each morning, Abram would stand and sniff the air, so to speak, trying to discern which direction they would go

---

31 Zornberg, Aviva G. *The Beginning of Desire: Reflections on Genesis*. (New York. 1995). "An act of radical discontinuity is, it seems, depicted in the Torah as the essential basis for all continuity: for that act of birth that will engender the body and the soul of a new kind of nation—their *akarut*, in its double sense of infertility and rootlessness—is placed in a context of ultimate blessing (Genesis 12:2).

32 Genesis 12.1-3

33 Rambam, Genesis 12.1: "To the land that I will show you": he wandered aimlessly from nation to nation and kingdom to kingdom, till he reached Canaan, when God said to him, "To your seed I shall give this land" (12.7). This was the fulfillment of "to the land that I will show you" and therefore he settled there...Before that, he did not yet know that that land was the subject of the command...That is why he later said to Abimelech, "God made me wander from my father's house" (Genesis 20.13). For indeed he wandered like a lost lamb."

that day. Sometimes he would decide that they would have to retrace their steps. Sarai didn't complain. She saw that the journey not the destination was important. Both of them knew a peace they had not known in years. God, someone Other, seemed to engage them in what they came to call the in-between spaces that existed in the narrow corners of their mind, in the depths of their feelings, and in the confined spaces of their vision. At special moments of clarity they heard the voices of future generations: "They wander about without food."[34] "I have gone astray like a lost sheep."[35]

The questions in Abram's mind did not cease with his physical wandering. From childhood he had wandered in his mind with question after question. His feet now resembled his mind. They too came to dead ends, and like his mind, they kept moving. How many dead ends must one reach before one knows the way! When he thought he had found the way, he discovered that another door was opening, and yet another door. But each entrance was a new encounter with the Other who he was now beginning to address as Thou. Sarai could see a daily change in him. One day she said to him, "I see that your answers are but landing pads that propel take-off into further and deeper questions." She was proud of her husband. He too needed her support to keep traveling on his dangerous intellectual journey that he knew would alienate him more and more from others who wouldn't be able to accept his findings. He reminded Sarai that they would be a blessing to all their descendants so they must keep searching and wandering. Often when he was in deep distress, God spoke to him and said, "Fear not. I am!"

Arrival in Canaan

It had been a particularly tiring day. Not only were Abram and Sarai dragging their feet, so were the animals. As they looked for a camping site, Abram and Sarai suddenly stopped in their tracks, faced each other and said in one voice, "Canaan!" They both knew at the same time that Canaan was their destination. They could hardly wait for the morning and before they knew it, they had crossed the border into Canaan. They passed through the land as far as the site of Shechem. When they reached the Oak of Moreh, Abram's feet grounded. He couldn't lift them for he felt glued to the earth. He lifted his eyes and saw God! God spoke to him, "I will give this land to your offspring." Abram couldn't answer. Instead he built an altar to YAH "who had appeared to him".

---

34 Job 38.41
35 Psalm 19.17

This was the beginning of a whole series of dramatic events. They left almost immediately for the hill country surrounding Bethel. There Abram built another altar but this time he invoked God by name! Sarai heard him speaking intimately with God. She smiled to herself. This man of hers who had sought God all his life was at this moment able to address God by name. YAH, he had said. She knew that Name had to do with the verb *to be*. She whispered to herself, "Yah! Being. Is-Was-Will Be. Yah!"

Sarai didn't let on that she had heard; instead she helped to prepare for their next destination. They set out towards the Negev. She didn't know that this time she was going to be tested. Because there was no food, they had to continue to Egypt. In order to protect her husband from death, she ended up in Pharaoh's palace. Pharaoh was smitten by her beauty and wanted her for his mistress. She accepted to go to the palace because her own experience of God told her that she would be protected. God did not let her down. Pharaoh was unable to touch her. Abram and Sarai and Lot left Egypt rich with animals and possessions.

When they arrived back at Bethel, the herdsmen of Abram and Lot quarreled over the land because it could not support both of their flocks and herds. Abram said to Lot, "Let there be no strife between you and me, and between your herders and my herders; for we are kindred. Separate yourself from me. If you take the left hand, then I will go to the right; or if you take the right hand, then I will go to the left." Lot looked about him, and saw that the plain of the Jordan was well watered everywhere so he chose the plain and moving eastward, he settled near Sodom. Many wicked people lived there.

Abram settled in the land of Canaan. After Lot had separated from him, YHWH said to Abram, "Raise your eyes. All the land that you see I will give to you and to your offspring forever. I will make your offspring like the dust of the earth. Rise up, walk through the length and the breadth of the land, for I will give it to you." So Abram moved his tent, and came and settled by the oaks of Mamre, which were at Hebron.

An Awesome Encounter

One day God spoke again to Abram, "Do not be afraid, Abram, I am your shield; your reward shall be very great." Abram cried out, "O Lord GOD, what will you give me, for I continue childless, and Eliezer, a slave born in my house is to be my heir." YHWH said to him. No one but your very own issue shall be your heir. Your descendants shall be countless as the stars of heaven."

The sun was going down. Suddenly Abram felt weary and he fell into a deep sleep. A deep and terrifying darkness descended upon him such as he had never known before. What happened to him at that moment is not known but afterwards it was written of him:

> What is this condition of right love? It is, that one should love God with an excessive, powerful love, till one's soul is totally involved in love of God, and one is constantly obsessed (*shoge*, mad) by it, as though ill with love sickness, when there is no place in one's mind free of the love of that woman with whom one is obsessed—neither when one sits nor stands, eats nor drinks. More than this, should be the love of God in the heart of those who love Him and are obsessed by Him. This is the meaning of the command, "You shall love your God with all your heart and with all your soul and with all your might." And " I am love-sick."[36]

The intimacy of that moment led to a change of name. God took an "H" from the divine name of YHWH and inserted it into Abram's name so that it now read, Abraham, meaning the "Father of a Throng of Nations." God added the same letter to Sarai's name to read Sarah, Princess, meaning that she would become the mother of a multitude. Abraham was now ninety-nine years old and Sarah was ninety.

There is no Impression without Expression

1. "Go forth." "Go to yourself." "Become what you are." When you are dissatisfied, move. It is not as important to know the direction as to move, i.e., a stalled car.

What do you want to change in your life and what are you afraid to change? A soldier asked his commander, "Which direction should I go?" The commander answered, "Always follow the sounds of battle."

2.Abraham told Abimelech that God caused him to wander from his father's house (Genesis 20.13). God *caused* him to wander! God wanted Abraham to get lost for only the lost person finds God. How will you start your journey trusting that God will take you where you need to go? Buber says that

---

36   Rambam, *Mishneh Torah, Hilkhot Teshuva* 10.3

every encounter involves sacrifice and risk.

3.Abram was a man obsessed with God. He had the one obsession allowed to humans: "Love the Lord your God with all your heart, and with all your soul, and with all your might." How would you lead your life if you were obsessed with God? Who is the holiest person you ever met? What made them that way? Was it worth it?

5. Buber said that I-Thou relationships do not make life easier but rather harder, harder with meaning. What are you willing to give up to have a life of meaning? What are you willing to do? Sacrifice is giving up. Risk is what you do. Abraham sacrificed his homeland, his family, his business, and he went blind into another country. One's last frontier is facing the unknown in one's own life.

Hagar and Ishmael. *Gustave Dore*

4.

GUESTS AT THE TABLE

As we converse with each other, we also speak to God in the Eternal Thou.

Genesis
Vayera
18:1 – 22:24

ABRAHAM AND SARAH continued to live by the oaks of Mamre, at Hebron. They loved to have people over for a meal. Not only did they get news of near and far away places, but something always seemed to happen when they were joyfully and peacefully eating together. Life's problems were eased; pain was lessened, and the light seemed brighter. Was it the smell of roasting meat, the aroma of freshly baked bread, and the glow of burning embers that lifted their spirits? They didn't know. What they did know was the warm Presence that filled their hearts when they sat together with others at a festive meal. Yes, they all ate routine meals but when the routine meal was changed to a festive meal heaven felt even closer. The physical act of exquisite dining opened the door to Presence.

A Frugal Meal becomes a Banquet

But today Abraham wasn't speaking. His pain was too great. After God changed their names to Abraham and Sarah, God commanded Abraham, "This is my covenant, which you shall keep, between me and you and your offspring after you: 'Every male among you shall be circumcised. You shall circumcise the flesh of your foreskins, and it shall be a sign of the covenant between me and you.'" Abraham winced but he did as God commanded. He was ninety-nine years old.

Sarah felt sorry for him as she watched him sitting at the entrance of the tent, in the hottest part of the day, peering into the distance, his face creased with pain. She brought him a cup of sweetened black tea but before she reached him, he jumped up and ran out the door. She couldn't understand how he could move and now there he was speaking to three strangers. She heard him saying, "My lords, pray if I have found favor in your eyes, pray do not pass by your servant! Pray let a little water be fetched, then wash your feet and recline under the tree; let me fetch you a bit of bread, that you may refresh your hearts, then afterward you may pass on—for you have, after all, passed your servant's way!"

The strangers agreed to stop. Abraham became oblivious to his pain. He had promised a meal to these strangers. He moved quickly from here to there. He hastened towards Sarah and said, "Hurry! Three measures of choice flour! Knead it, make bread-cakes!" And he himself actually ran to the oxen and fetched a young ox, tender and fine, and gave it to a serving-lad, that he might hasten to make it ready; then he fetched cream and milk and the young ox. Such was the flurry of activity that in no time at all, the meal was ready.

During this time the strangers have had their feet washed and were relaxing comfortably enjoying the teasing aromas that filled the air. Abraham set the meal before them and stood under the tree in order to serve them according to the rules of politeness. It was not the promised spartan meal of a little water and a bit of bread that Abraham originally offered them but a gastronomic delight: newly baked bread, roasted ox, cream and milk and other goodies. Sarah was nowhere to be seen.

During the banquet one of the strangers asked, "Where is Sarah, your wife?" Unbeknown to Abraham, Sarah was listening at the entrance of the tent. She heard the question. Then she heard one of the visitors say, " I will return, yes, return to you when time revives, and Sarah your wife will have a son." Sarah unable to contain herself burst out laughing. She felt her soft hanging breasts and thought within herself, "After I have become old, is there to be pleasure for me? And my husband, he too is an old man!"

But the stranger, who is none other than YHWH, heard her and knowing her thoughts said to those around him, "Now why does Sarah laugh and say: 'Shall I really give birth, now that I am old?' Is anything beyond YHWH? I will return, at a set time, and Sarah will have a son." Sarah emerged into the light and said, "I didn't laugh." The stranger knowing that her son's name would be called Laughter looked directly at her and said, "Oh, yes, you did laugh." Sarah's heart was beating fast now but she said no more. She had a deep feeling that what was being said was about to happen though she wasn't aware that it was God who was actually addressing her at this moment.

The strangers got up to leave. Abraham accompanied them for the first part of their journey. After he waved them off and saw them turn in the direction of Sodom, he remained standing there. God saw him standing and said, "Shall I hide from Abraham what I am about to do, seeing that Abraham shall become a great and mighty nation, and all the nations of the earth shall be blessed in him? No, for I have chosen him." So God spoke to him and said, "How great is the outcry against Sodom and Gomorrah and how very grave their sin! I am about to destroy them."

Abraham was greatly disturbed, and said, "Will you indeed sweep away the righteous with the wicked? Suppose there are fifty righteous within the city, will you then sweep away the righteous with the wicked, so that the righteous fare as the wicked! Far be that from you! Shall not the Judge of all the earth do what is just?" And YHWH said, "If I find fifty righteous in the city of Sodom, I will forgive the whole place for their sake." Abraham answered, "Let me take it upon myself to speak to YHWH, I who am but dust and ashes. Suppose five of the fifty righteous are lacking? Will you destroy the whole city for lack of five?" And YHWH said, "I will not destroy it if I find forty-five there." Again he spoke to him, "Suppose forty are found there." YHWH answered, "For the sake of forty I will not do it." Then he said, "Oh do not be angry if I speak. Suppose thirty are found there." YHWH answered, "I will not do it, if I find thirty there." He said, "Let me take it upon myself to speak to you, YHWH. Suppose twenty are found there." YHWH answered, "For the sake of twenty I will not destroy it." Then he said, "Oh, do not be angry if I speak just once more. Suppose ten are found there." YHWH answered, "For the sake of ten I will not destroy it." Abraham said to himself, "I dare not bargain for less." Slowly he dragged his feet home. The pain of his circumcision returned in full force.

He told Sarah about his encounter with God and how he had argued with God to save the cities of Sodom and Gemorrah. Sarah tried to comfort him but he could not be comforted. All night long he tossed and turned so great was his agitation. He rose early the next morning and went to the place where he had stood with YHWH and looked down toward Sodom and Gomorrah. Not a building stood. He did not see a living person. Clouds of smoke rose to the sky like the smoke of a furnace. No one remained except for Lot and his two daughters. Abraham stood and wept. After long hours of weeping, Abraham returned to Sarah. Sarah tried to comfort him, yet before she knew it she unthinkingly said, "Do you think you should have bargained with God down to three?"

Abraham was startled by such a suggestion. Clasping his hand over his eyes he exclaimed, "You are right. Why didn't I? Why did I stop with ten? For one righteous person God would have saved the cities!"

Sarah said, "Abraham, you tried. Come. Let's go to bed. Remember what the man said, 'At the set time I will return to you, in due season, and Sarah shall have a son. Is anything too wonderful for YHWH?'" That night Abraham knew his wife and she became pregnant.

A Great Feast Indeed

Sarah's stomach swelled; her breasts filled out, her face lost its lines. In time, as promised by the visitors, she gave birth to a laughing boy whom they named Isaac. At the time of weaning they put on a great banquet, a great drinking feast. The laughter and the jokes abounded. Sarah could hardly take her eyes off her son. His birth was beyond anything she could have imagined. Once, when she thought she was too old to give birth, she gave her servant, Hagar, to Abraham to have a surrogate son for her. And Hagar had a son by Abraham whom she named, Ishmael.

When Hagar gave birth she foolishly and haughtily strutted before Sarah, as if to say, "I can do what you can't do."[37] Sarah suffered from her taunts.

When the guests were leaving the celebration for Isaac's weaning, Sarah looked out the window and saw Ishmael playing with her son, Isaac. She exploded. Confronting Abraham, she said, "Cast out this slave woman with her son; for the son of this slave woman shall not inherit along with my son Isaac." Abraham was very disturbed by these words. How could he throw Hagar out? How could she and her son survive? Then he thought that if she could survive, she would be better off than live under Sarah's thumb. God confirmed his thinking and said to him, "Do not be distressed because of the boy and because of your slave woman; whatever Sarah says to you, do as she tells you, for it is through Isaac that offspring shall be named for you. As for the son of the slave woman, I will make a nation of him also, because he is your offspring."

---

37 Genesis 16

With that, Abraham rose early in the morning, took bread and a skin of water and gave it to Hagar. He put it on her shoulder, along with the child, and sent her away.

Hagar goes from Ignominy to Glory

Hagar turned her back to Abraham and with her head held high marched forward. Once before Hagar had fled from Sarah. The first night, as she was hiding by a spring of water in the wilderness on the way to Shur, she heard a Voice, "Hagar, slave-girl of Sarai, where have you come from and where are you going?" She said, "I am running away from my mistress Sarai." The Voice said to her, "Return to your mistress, and submit to her. I have great news for you. You have conceived and you shall bear a son and you shall call his name Ishmael. He shall be great and his offspring shall be numerous as the stars in the sky." Hagar stood up and did what no one had ever done before. She gave God a new name. Reaching out her arms towards God, she said, "You are *El-roi*, the One who sees." And turning towards the spring she said, "You shall be called *Well of the Living One that sees me.*" Emboldened by what she had seen and done, she returned to Sarah. She took comfort in knowing that a child was growing within her. When she gave birth to Ishmael, Abram was eighty-six years old.

But now all was changed. Hagar did not leave on her own volition. Abraham cast her out at Sarah's instigation. She wandered with her son in the wilderness of Beer-Sheba. The gourd of water was empty. She searched and scratched among the scrubs for signs of a spring. The sun beat down cruelly on their heads. Finally dying of thirst, Hagar threw her child under one of the bushes so as not to see him die. She lifted up her voice and wailed. Ishmael also howled from the place where he was thrown. God took pity on them and from heaven sent Raphael, the healing angel, who said to Hagar,

> What ails you, Hagar? Do not be afraid,
> for God has heard the voice of the lad there where he is.
> Arise, lift up the lad and grasp him with your hand,
> for a great nation will God make of him!

Then Hagar opened her eyes and to her great astonishment saw a well of water. She quickly filled the skin with water and gave Ishmael to drink. And God was with the lad as he grew up.[38]

---

38 Genesis 21

Abraham is Tested

Unnoticed, HaSatan[39], the Adversary, was present at the great banquet that celebrated the weaning of Isaac. He was jealous of God's love for Abraham and that nations of the world would be blessed through him. So he went before God and said, "This old man – You granted him fruit of the womb when he was a hundred years old. And yet of all the banquets that he made, he did not have a single turtle dove or a young bird to sacrifice to you!" God said to him, "He has done nothing that was not for his son – and if I were to say to him, 'Sacrifice your son to me,' he would immediately obey." Right after that, God tested Abraham. God called to him, "Abraham." Abraham answered, "Here I am." God said, "Take your son, your only son Isaac, whom you love, and go to the land of Moriah, and offer him there as a burnt offering on one of the mountains that I shall show you."

Abraham was struck dumb. How would any of God's promises be fulfilled if Isaac were not! How would his posterity be as the stars in the sky and the dust of the earth if Isaac were not! Yet Abraham rose early the next morning while Sarah was still in a deep sleep, and cut the wood for the burnt offering. Then he saddled his donkey, and took two of his young men with him, and his son Isaac and set out for the mountain that God promised to show him. On the third day he looked up and saw the place far away. When he arrived he bound his son, put him on the altar and was about to sacrifice him when God called to him, "Abraham, Abraham!" And he said, "Here I am." God said, "Do not lay your hand on the boy or do anything to him. I will indeed bless you, and I will make your offspring as numerous as the stars of heaven and as the sand that is on the seashore." Abraham looked up and saw a ram caught in a thorn bush. He took the ram and offered it up instead of his son. He called the place, YHWH Yera'eh (YAH Sees).

Sarah is Tested

In the meantime, Sarah was distraught. Where was her beloved son, Isaac? Where was Abraham? Something was not right. For three days she searched for Isaac. When she reached Kiriath-arba (that is, Hebron), she was weary, distraught and frazzled. "Something has happened to him, I know," she wailed. Then HaSatan came to her and said, "Do you know what your old man has done? He has taken your son Isaac, whom you love, and has mur-

---

39 Sanhedrian 89b: "After these events": after the words of Satan, as it is written, "The child grew up and was weaned, and (Abraham) held a great feast" (21:8).

dered him." At those words, Sarah's soul departed from her. She was one hundred and twenty seven years old.

There is no Impression without Expression

1."And the Lord appeared." Every appearance of God is a moment of decision. Every encounter is perceived as mission. Our response is, "Here I am" and "Thy will be done by me whom you need." Examples: Abraham, Tobit, Jesus. What will you do for God *today*?

2. A banquet is stepping into the presence of God and out of the world. Amy Tan[40] in her novel, *The Joy Luck Club*, describes how a group of women who called themselves the Joy Luck Club held a party once a week to raise their spirits[41]. People thought they were possessed to celebrate when so many in their families were at that moment suffering. "It's not that we had no heart for pain," she wrote, but "to despair was to sit back for something already lost. Or to prolong what was already unbearable."

To despair over something that has happened is to live in the past, like guilt is in the past and remorse is in the past. Paradoxically, worrying about the future is also living in the past. The Joy Luck Club put the women into the present and they took the presence with them into the rest of the week.

What is the difference between a "fast food" snack and a meal with friends?

3. Try to see, *Babette's Feast*, a video adaptation of a short story by Isak Dinesen, which is an account of an event of transformation of twelve dinner guests of two elderly sisters in a little Danish town. The story centers on Babette, an exile who arrives at the home of the two spinster daughters of the founder of an extremely grim Christian group. For twelve years Babette faithfully served the sisters and continued to prepare for them their bland meals of ale-bread soup and dried flaked cod. Eventually, Babette became rich on a forgotten lottery ticket and begged the sisters that she might pre-

---

40   Amy Tan. *The Joy Luck Club* (New York. 1989).

41   Amy Tan is an American of Chinese extraction. The novel opens with the mother describing the origin of the Joy Luck Club, which she invented in order to survive the terrors of the invasion of her hometown in China. She wrote: "I thought up Joy Luck on a summer night that was so hot even the moths fainted to the ground…At all hours of the day and night, I heard screaming sounds, I didn't know if it was a peasant slitting the throat of a runaway pig or an officer beating a half-dead peasant for lying in his way on the sidewalk."

pare a dinner in honor of their late father's hundredth birthday. She further asked as a favor to pay for it with her winnings. Since she had never asked for a thing, the sisters reluctantly agreed. But as the provisions begin to arrive, the dinner guests watched in fear from behind their shutters convinced that the meal was a sinful excess, and so they vowed to merely sample each course, out of devotion to the sisters and a sense of Christian charity and compassion, and they further vowed neither to taste nor speak of what they ate and drank. Since the minister's death, schisms and cliques had developed in the community and members were behaving badly towards each other. When the evening of the anniversary finally arrived, they all filed gloomily into the dining room but the magic of the moment begins to work on their cold hearts. Gradually, old feuds were forgotten, debts forgiven, and love rekindled. Of that night, Dinesen wrote:

> Of what happened later in the evening nothing definite can here be stated. None of the guests later on had any clear remembrance of it. They only knew that the rooms had been filled with a heavenly light, as if a number of small halos had blended into one glorious radiance...Long after midnight the windows of the house shone like gold and golden song flowed out into the winter air.[42]

Do you remember a golden night?

---

42 Dinesan, Isak. *Babette's Feast and Other Anecdotes of Destiny* (New York, 1988).

Eliezer meets Rebekah. *Gustave Dore*

5.

INNATE KNOWING

All real living is meeting.

Genesis
Hayei Sarah
23:1- 25:18

ABRAHAM KNEW THAT in another two hours he would be home and would have to explain to Sarah why he stealthily disappeared with Isaac. He had been gone three days. Would she understand! What did she do when she discovered we were gone and didn't return! These questions and others swirled around in his head as he walked. The constant rhythm of his feet trampling the stones and gravel brought back the recent memories of his outward journey to the mountain over this same path. "How long and horrible these last three days have been! Surely the longest and most horrible of my life," he whispered to himself. He relived his past emotional turmoil and conflicting emotions in the face of unanswerable questions: How would he be blessed with posterity if his son were dead? How could God make such demands on him? Had God really spoken to him or was it HaSatan, his fragmented self? With the exit of hope and impenetrable darkness invading his soul, he heard the Voice, "Do not lay your hand on the boy or do anything to him. I will indeed bless you."

Coming around a mound, he looked up and saw his home from afar. He quickened his steps to a near run.

When he arrived, she was not there! Something was wrong! "Oh, God," he cried, "Where is she?" Madly, he went searching for her. When he reached Hebron he learned that Sarah had died. The villagers led him to the place of her death. When he set his eyes on her crumpled form, stretched out on a mat, he sank to the ground beside her. Crushed with sorrow, he tore the lapel on his shirt and sobbed and sobbed. When he had no more tears left, he arose and went to Ephron, the Hittite, and bought from him the cave of Machpelah and there he buried Sarah.

After the burial, Abraham felt very tired and old. Sensing that death would soon claim him, he called for his servant Eliezer and said to him, "I do not want my son Isaac to marry a Canaanite woman from here. Go therefore to the country from which I came, to my family who live in Nahor, near Haron, in northern Mesopotamia, a country also known as Aram-Naharayim (Aram of two rivers) and get a wife for my son Isaac."

Eliezer knew it was a five hundred mile journey. He wondered how he could convince a woman to leave home and come with him, a stranger, to a foreign land! "Master," he said, "what if, when I find the woman, she refuses to come with me? Should I take Isaac back with me?"

"No, never," replied Abraham. "God who brought me here from there will bless you. God will send an angel before you and help you along the way. Here, take this," Abraham said, as he stretched out his hand and took a document[43] he had just written and handed it to Eliezer. When Eliezer opened the document he saw that it was a promissory note bequeathing all of Abraham's possessions to Isaac. Eliezer smiled and tucked it into his satchel. He thought to himself "This is all the power I need." Taking his leave of Abraham, he chose ten of his master's best camels and set out for Aram-Naharaim, to the city of Nahor.

Rebekah—Abraham's Grandniece.

Back in Nahor, as Rebekah was growing up, she heard different stories about Abraham, her great uncle. She felt close to him though she didn't know him. One day while she was helping her mother prepare the evening meal of salads, pita bread, humous and hot tea, she asked, "Mother, I am your daughter and that of my father, Bethuel. My father is the son of Milcah, the wife of Nahor who is Abraham's brother. What relation am I to Abraham? Tell me what you know about him."

From the dreadful tales she heard about Abraham smashing the idols in his father's shop, Rebekah wanted to know more about him for she, too, could not relate to the idols of stone with their strange faces. She had grown fond of a

---

43 A *kol tuv* (all his master's goodness) in his hand.

carob tree some distance from the house. Here she found comfort and protection from the boys and men when they were on the prowl for girls and young women. She herself had not been molested. This was strange for she knew that she was considered one of the most beautiful women in the extended family and she often saw men looking at her in a way that made her uncomfortable.

She looked into her mother's face for a response. She noted that today her mother looked particularly tired. The skin on her face was wrinkled like the cracked and dry mud of a dry wadi. Suddenly her mother who felt uncomfortable with her daughter staring at her, answered, "You are his grandniece. You are just like him. He was a man in a hurry. He had a mind of his own. He was always searching and asking questions. He didn't believe in our household gods. Every day he seemed to have a new god. First it was the sun, then it was the moon One day he heard voices that told him to leave here with his wife Sarah, who was barren. No one has heard from him since." Catching a faint smile on Rebekah's face, she added, "I hope you are not hearing Voices!"

No, Rebekah didn't hear voices but she had a strong feeling of what she wanted and didn't want, not like the other women she knew who never questioned or imagined that their lives could be different. She felt compelled to choose life rather than be lived by it. Her body was her guide. When she was questioned on hasty decisions she made, she would often reply by putting her hands on her stomach and say, "I just feel that it is right—I feel it here in my gut!" Nothing stopped her. She spoke to people who were strangers. She helped those in need. Her brother, Laban, often challenged her on what he called her "wayward ways." Often he would say, "You belong to our family. Don't lower yourself by talking to tramps." Each time, she would laugh and answer, "I will make you rich some day."

Eliezer meets Rebekah at the Well.

Exhausted, with dust covering him from foot to head, with face unshaven and soiled clothes, Eliezer arrived in town towards evening with his desert-weary thirsty camels. When he saw the daughters of the townspeople coming to the well to draw water he prayed: "O LORD, God of my master Abraham, please grant me success today and show steadfast love to my master Abraham. Let the young woman to whom I shall say, 'Please offer your jar that I may drink,' and who shall say, 'Drink, and I will water your camels'—let her be the one whom you have appointed for your servant Isaac. By this I shall know that you have shown steadfast love to my master." He prayed thus because he didn't trust his intuition to intuit the right woman and he needed signs.

When Rebekah came up from the spring with her jar full of water on her shoulders, he ran to meet her and said, "Please let me sip a little water from your jar."

The other women were watching her. Would she let this tramp, who might even carry some disease, drink from her jar. Rebekah paid no heed to their looks but regarding the stranger she said, "Drink, my lord." She quickly lowered her jar upon her hand and gave him a drink. After he had drunk, she said, "I will draw for your camels also, until they have finished drinking."

When Rebekah made that decision she was not thinking of the huge capacity of a camel for water. One camel can drink as much as 100 liters of water at a time. Instead, she went into action. Like a nonstop blur of motion, down the steps and up again, she carried water to all his ten camels in her single jar until all were satisfied.

When the camels had finished drinking, the man took a gold nose-ring weighing a half shekel, and two bracelets for her arms weighing ten gold shekels, and said, "Tell me whose daughter you are. Is there room in your father's house for us to spend the night?" Without reticence, and to the horror of the women standing about, she accepted his gifts. Looking him straight in the eye, she liked what she saw, and she replied, "We have plenty of straw and fodder and a place to spend the night."

Rebekah ran home and told the family what she had done. When Laban, her brother, saw all the gold the stranger had given her, he ran out to the spring to meet Eliezer. "Come in, O blessed of the LORD. Why do you stand outside when I have prepared the house and a place for the camels?" So the man came into the house; and Laban unloaded the camels, and gave him straw and fodder for the camels, and water to wash his feet and the feet of the men who were with him. Then food was set before him to eat; but he said, "I will not eat until I have told my errand."

The Bride Price

Eliezer went into a lengthy retelling of all that happened to him since the beginning. He changed elements of the story to fit the situation. He brandished before their eyes the promissory note he held in his hand. "I am Abraham's servant," he said. "YAH has blessed my lord exceedingly, so that he has become great, he has given him sheep and oxen, silver and gold, servants and maids, camels and donkeys. Sarah, my lord's wife, bore my lord a son after she had grown old, and he has given him all that is his."

When Eliezer had finished speaking, Laban and Bethuel said together, "The thing comes from the LORD; we cannot speak to you anything bad or good. Look, Rebekah is before you, take her and go, and let her be the wife of your master's son, as the LORD has spoken."

When Eliezer heard their words, he brought out jewelry of silver and of gold, and elegant and costly garments, and gave them to Rebekah; he also gave to her brother and to her mother costly ornaments. Then Rebekah and her mother left. The servants who had been preparing a special meal set it before the men and they ate the food and drank the wine.

Rebekah was not upset that her father and her mother had just sold her to Eliezer to be married to a man she had never seen. Her body already knew that was what she wanted to do. While her mother went into the back room, Rebekah went out to visit the camels that were all lying down now. She felt a particular kinship with these lonely ships of the desert. As she walked among them they lifted their heads and moaned and bawled but these sounds were not frightening but pleasant to her ears. Though their ears were small, she knew that their acute hearing made them aware of her light step and even perhaps her thoughts. She felt the hump on their backs which a few hours ago had been soft and flabby for lack of sustenance during the long trek from there to here. "Eat lots," she said softly to them. "Get those humps back up. You'll be carrying me away from here before long."

Morning came early. The men were stirring. She heard Eliezer arguing with her mother and her brother who were saying, "Let the girl remain with us a while, at least ten days; after that she may go." But he said to them, "Do not delay me, since YAH has made my journey successful; let me go that I may go to my master."

They said, "We will call the girl, and ask her."

Rebekah smiled. She said to herself, "They didn't bother consulting me about my marriage and now they consult me over a ten day extension of time. Why? They want more gifts!"

Her brother said to her, "Will you go with this man?"

She said, "I will."

Encounter with Isaac

With that Rebekah and her nurse mounted the camels. The camels ambled along at about 3 miles per hour, covering about 25 miles a day. So the journey was long and tiring but Rebekah didn't mind. She eagerly ate up all that Eliezer told her about Abraham and Sarah and their son, Isaac. As the twentieth day approached, Rebekah had mixed feelings inside her. She felt she would recognize Isaac when she saw him. But would he be handsome? Would she love him? Yes, she knew she would. Then she saw a man walking towards them as evening was drawing near. She knew it was he. She called to Eliezer and asked, "Who is the man over there, walking in the field to meet us?" Eliezer said, "It is my master." She slipped quickly from the camel and took her veil and covered herself. Glancing at the sun she marked its position in the sky. Today was Friday and Sabbath would begin shortly.

Isaac and Eliezer stood talking at a distance. Eliezer told Isaac all the things that he had done. When Isaac was satisfied with what he heard, he came slowly towards Rebekah. They didn't embrace but a warm feeling passed between them. He took her and brought her into his mother's tent.

Her first act upon entering the tent was to find the Sabbath candles. She learned about Sabbath observance from Eliezer and its importance to Isaac. Seeing that the sun was about to set she lit the Sabbath candles. She paused for a moment, held her hands over the light and drew the light into herself. Then she hurriedly washed and changed her clothes. She was beaming as she reappeared before Isaac. She stood before him and looked at him.

She was not disappointed in what she saw. She knew how Sarah loved him, how he was brought up in a supportive environment while she, in contrast, knew the world, knew its limitations and its hardships. Isaac knew evil only from afar, she thought, while I know it from close up. All her life she had tried to adhere to what was good. It would be easier now, she thought, in this environment.

As they sat down together at the Sabbath table, the *Shechinah*, God's presence, which had departed at the death of his mother, returned. A warm heavenly glow spread throughout their dwelling.

There is no Impression without Expression

1. This parashah begins not with the words, "the death of Sarah," but with the words, "the life of Sarah." What evidence do you see of Sarah's continued influence in this parashah? Note that Abraham buys a burial place for Sarah and settles down, that is, he becomes tied to the land. Note also that Abraham wants Isaac to have a wife like Sarah. What are the implications for Isaac that he continued to live in his mother's tent, and what are the implications for Rebekah?

2. We have all had a beloved person die. Do you feel that person is still with you? How does that person continue to affect your life?

3. Rebekah met God through her body. What messages does your body give you about the relationships in your life? Who made you blush? Who made you cry? Who made you laugh? Who made your blood pressure skyrocket? Who made your pulse race? Who made you feel pity, compassion, mercy?

What did you do with these gut reactions? Did you obey your body? Sometimes people say "my heart told me one thing but my mind told me another." What does this statement mean?

Should you listen to your heart or your head? In an I-Thou encounter the two are united because we answer with our whole being.

4. There are people who follow the beaten path. There are people who follow a voice even when it takes them across the beaten path of protesting others. When did you not play it safe?

5. When Isaac is meditating in the field, Rebekah asks, "Who is that man?" Isaac lifts his eyes. He sees Rebekah. Their eyes meet. It was the right moment at the right place. Has this happened to you?

Isaac blesses Jacob. *Gustave Dore*

6.

ENCOUNTERING THE OTHER

A person's will to profit and to be powerful have their natural and proper effect so long as they are linked with, and upheld by one's will to enter into relation.

REBEKAH WAS ALONE reminiscing over the past several years of her life with Isaac and his family. She had just said goodbye to Isaac who left to bury his father who died the previous day at the age of one hundred seventy-five years old.

Genesis
Toledot
25:19 –28:9

She remembered her first meeting with Abraham and his wife, Keturah. How excited she had been! And how she had wanted to meet Keturah! Before that first visit, she spent hours with Isaac asking him thousands of questions about his family. She still recalled the horror she felt when she learned that her admired uncle, Abraham, had cast out Hagar and her son, Ishmael, because of his mother's fears. Her belief was restored, however, when Isaac told her how his father went searching for Hagar after Sarah died and married her[44]. "He gave her the name of Keturah, a Hebrew word that means 'attached' (ketar)," Isaac explained. "My father remained attached to Hagar and Ishmael. He always asked himself if God had truly told him to expel Hagar or whether or not he had been a coward in the face of my mother's anger. Yet others say that the name means *incense* because Hagar's deeds were as pleasant as incense (*ketorot*)."

While Rebekah was reminiscing about the past, Isaac and Ishmael, who had become reconciled through their father's marriage with Keturah, buried

---

44   Rashi, Genesis 25.1

Abraham in the cave of Machpelah in Hebron where Abraham had buried his first wife, Sarah. When the burial rites were over, Ishmael embraced Isaac and returned home. He was now rich partly because of the gifts bestowed upon him by Abraham when he married his mother. Isaac went to Beer-lahai-roi to Rebekah. He wept as he walked for the loss of his father. He also wept because he and Rebekah had no children. He was forty when he married her. Now he was sixty. As he neared home, an insistent hope within him burst into prayer: "Oh, Yah, God," he pleaded, "Give us a child."

Meanwhile, while Isaac was invoking God for a child, Rebekah was still sitting a few hundred meters from their home, amongst the thick arms of her favourite carob tree, thinking about her own barrenness. She was told she was barren but since she and Isaac were a monogamous couple, could not Isaac be the one who was infertile! Why did people presume it was she! "If only I had a child," she whispered, "I would enfold this new life within me as the leaves and branches of this tree are enfolding me now." She was awakened from her reverie by Isaac's voice calling her. She slid to the ground and ran towards him. They sat for long hours talking together. That night Rebekah conceived. God heard the prayer of Isaac and the dream of Rebekah.

A Difficult Pregnancy

The joy of being pregnant was fraught with pain. As her stomach enlarged, Rebekah felt torn apart. At any moment of the day or night, pain stabbed her, as though a battle was going on within her. At certain moments her womb rocked with the turmoil within. She never told Isaac about her pain nor the number of times when the pain became unbearable, nor that at times she wished she were dead. He was a peace loving man who loved to stay at home, dig his wells and take care of his flocks.

One day in the third month of her pregnancy, sure she was going to be torn asunder, she ran to her carob tree. Swinging into her usual position and grasping the branches on either side, she screamed out to God, "If it is to be this way, why do I live? Answer me, please." Yah heard her scream and spoke to her, "Two nations are in your womb, and two peoples born of you shall be divided; the one shall be stronger than the other, the elder shall serve the younger."

Rebekah was astounded. This was the first time that she, unlike her great uncle, Abraham, actually heard a Voice talking to her. Hagar had also heard God's voice in this place, by this carob tree, near this well. "Two nations in my womb," she repeated, "and the elder shall serve the younger!" She met

Isaac at the door when she returned but she didn't tell him her secret for could anyone believe what she had just heard!

Esau and Jacob

The time came for Rebekah to give birth. The first child came out reddish and covered with a mantle of hair so they named him Esau because of his physical appearance. Afterwards his brother came out, his hand clutching Esau's heel, so they named him Jacob, meaning heel.

The boys grew up quickly. Esau became a skilful hunter, a man of the field. Isaac loved him. He was a hairy, energetic, thoughtful man. He often brought succulent game for his father to eat.

Jacob, unlike his brother in appearance, was smooth-skinned and tall. He loved to stay home, which of course, pleased his mother, who knew that this son had a special mission. He loved to cook and he loved to study Torah. Those who spoke about him called him the academic, which for some was a pejorative term.

One day, when Jacob was cooking a stew, Esau came in famished and said, "Pray give me a gulp of the red-stuff, that red-stuff, for I am so weary!" Jacob, the smooth skinned man, perhaps envious of his hairy macho brother who was the favourite of his father, replied, "Sell me your firstborn-right here-and-now." To his surprise, Esau, who was much stronger, did not grab for the food, but said, "Here, I am on my way to dying, so what good to me is a firstborn-right?" Jacob said, "Swear to me here-and-now." So Esau swore to him and sold him his birthright. And Jacob gave him bread and lentil stew. Esau ate and drank and went on his way.

Jacob Encounters Life

The years passed. Rebekah was fond of her son, Jacob. She knew he was the one who would carry on the family heritage. Isaac was fond of his son Esau, who was conspicuously the opposite of him. Isaac was a man who let things happen to him. Though he was a young man he did not struggle with his father when he tied him to the altar to be slain. He did not go out to find himself a wife. A wife was brought to him. Unlike his father who was a wanderer, he stayed more or less in one place. He re-dug the wells his father dug; he settled the land and became rich in herds of sheep and goats. His hope for the future lay with Esau who was forceful and active, a hunter, a free man, and a man of the open fields.

One day, feeling old and with more difficulty than usual in seeing, Isaac called Esau and said to him, "My son!" and he answered, "Here I am." "See, I am old," Isaac explained, "I do not know the day of my death. Now then, take your weapons, your quiver and your bow, and go out to the field and hunt game for me. Then prepare for me savory food, such as I like, and bring it to me to eat, so that I may bless you before I die." Esau took leave of his father and went to the field to hunt for game, which he would prepare and bring to him.

Rebekah overheard the conversation and called her son, Jacob. She said to him, "I heard your father say to your brother Esau, 'Bring me game, and prepare for me savory food to eat, that I may bless you before the Lord before I die.' Now therefore, my son, obey my word as I command you. Go to the flock, and get me two choice kids, so that I may prepare from them savory food for your father, such as he likes; and you shall take it to your father to eat, so that he may bless you before he dies."

Jacob was afraid to take that step though he envied his brother. So he said to his mother, Rebekah, "Look, my brother Esau is a hairy man, and I am a man of smooth skin. Perhaps my father will feel me, and I shall seem to be mocking him, and bring a curse on myself and not a blessing."

Rebekah was born into a tough family and quickly learned that she must wheel and deal in order to survive. That meant getting one's hands dirty. Only those who withdrew from the world could remain innocent and pure. Looking into the innocent eyes of Jacob, she said, "Let your curse be on me, my son; only obey my word, and go, get them for me."

So Jacob went and caught two young goats and brought them to his mother; and his mother prepared savory food, such as his father loved. Then she took the best garments of her elder son Esau, which were with her in the house, and put them on her younger son Jacob. She put the skins of the kids on his hands and on the smooth part of his neck. She handed the savory food, and the bread that she had prepared, to her son Jacob and said, "Go, my son. Be not afraid."

Jacob was terrified. Would he receive a curse or a blessing? Whichever it was, he knew that once he crossed the threshold and stepped into his father's presence in the persona of his brother Esau, his life would be forever changed. He thought of all of the personalities he knew through his studies. He despised those who stood at the door and waited for someone to open it for them. He did not want to live a useless and boring life because he was afraid to go forward. He envied his brother, so full of libidinous energy, who was not afraid to face life and enjoy the wide-open fields. His father was too passive for him. He preferred to be like his mother who was a decisive woman, not afraid to make decisions, not afraid to go off into the unknown with a stranger to meet a man in a strange country and marry him. What voice did she listen to? He needed to step out of the door and just GO. Yes, he wanted what his brother had. He wanted the blessing destined for him. Kissing his mother he shut the door behind him and stepped into his father's presence.

"My father," he said to him.
"Here I am; who are you, my son?"
"I am Esau your firstborn. I have done as you told me; now sit up and eat of my game, so that you may bless me."
"How is it that you have found it so quickly, my son?"
"Because the Lord your God granted me success." He stressed your God and not *our* God because he was feeling guilty about the deception.

Isaac peered at his son to examine him, for doubts had crossed his mind. But the face before him was blurred in darkness. So he said, "Come near, that I may feel you, my son, to know whether you are really my son Esau or not."

Jacob turned pale as he stepped forward. His father reached out and caught his hairy hands. "The voice is Jacob's voice, but the hands are the hands of Esau." He was about to bless him and he paused, "Are you really my son, Esau?"

Jacob replied, "I am."

Lowering his hand, Isaac said, "Bring me the food you have prepared that I may eat it and bless you." Jacob brought it to him, and he ate; and he brought him wine, and he drank.

Then Isaac said to him, "Come near and kiss me, my son."

So Jacob drew near again and kissed him. As he leaned over his father, Isaac once again touched Esau's clothes. Emanating from them was the sweet smell of grass and dew and wind not the usual foul smell of goats and blood and decaying flesh. God approved! Raising his hand, Isaac prayed:

> May God give you of the dew of heaven, and of the fatness of
> the earth, and plenty of grain and wine. Let peoples serve you,

and nations bow down to you. Be master over your brothers. Cursed be everyone who curses you, and blessed be everyone who blesses you!"

Hearing steps at the door, Jacob fled, satisfied that he had obtained the blessing of the first-born. Esau entered and said," Let my father sit up and eat of his son's game, so that you may bless me." His father Isaac said to him, "Who are you?" He answered, "I am your firstborn son, Esau."

Isaac trembled violently, and said, "Who was it then that hunted game and brought it to me, and I ate it all before you came, and I have blessed him?— yes, and blessed he shall be!"

And Esau lifted up his voice and wept and cried out, "Is he not rightly named Jacob? For he has supplanted me these two times. He took away my birthright; and look, now he has taken away my blessing." Then he said, "Have you not reserved a blessing for me?" His father replied, "I have already made him your lord, and I have given him all his brothers as servants."

Now Esau hated Jacob even more because of the blessing with which his father had blessed him. He said, "I will break this yoke of my brother around my neck. As soon as the days of mourning for my father's death are over, I will kill him."

Rebekah ran to her son Jacob and said, "Your brother Esau is consoling himself by planning to kill you. Now therefore, my son, obey my voice; flee at once to my brother Laban in Haran, and stay with him a while, until your brother's fury turns away— until your brother's anger against you turns away, and he forgets what you have done to him; then I will send, and bring you back from there. Why should I lose both of you in one day?" With those words, Rebekah went to her husband and convinced him that he should send Jacob back to her brother, Laban, and take one of his daughters as wife. Isaac agreed. He called Jacob, blessed him and sent him away. Jacob left immediately on foot for the five hundred mile journey, not knowing the way nor daring to take time to pack.

There is no Impression without Expression

1. The story of Isaac and Rebekah and their two children Esau and Jacob (Genesis 26.34-28.9), is a story of flawed relationships. Each scene in the drama consists of a dialogue between two people: (1) Isaac—Esau; (2) Rebekah—Jacob; (3) Jacob—Isaac; (4) Isaac—Esau; (5) Rebekah—Jacob; (6) Rebekah—Isaac; and (7) Isaac—Jacob. Husband and wife do not talk to

each other until the penultimate scene, and there is no dialogue at all between the two brothers in this section. Rivalry, deceit, dishonesty, competition, compulsiveness, blindness, pain and suffering are all present. In other words, this is a dysfunctional family.

Rebekah is a great woman. Rebekah committed great sins. Many of the great women and men in the bible sinned grievously. Yet God loved them. God loved Moses. God loved David. God loved Ruth. God loved Sarah. Do you remember a time when you manipulated someone for his or her own good? Have you ever been manipulated for your own good? How did you feel? How did it turn out? When you manipulate another are you treating that person as a person or a thing?

2. Goatskins are important in this story. Jacob, dressed in the goatskin clothes of Esau, looks like a satyr, a goat God. In a sense, he is a goat God, both divine and human, capable of both noble and ignominious acts. In the end, the smelly goatskins give off a refreshing aroma, which causes Jacob to exclaim, "Ah, the smell of my son is like the smell of a field that the Lord has blessed." How do you account for this?

3.This is also a story about crossing thresholds, leaving the known for the unknown. Jacob stepped out of his mother's tent and walked into the presence of his father, not knowing if he would be cursed or blessed. He got what he wanted but he also got his hands dirty through deceit, which forced him to cross another threshold and flee from his country.

Some people refuse to cross thresholds. They fear the unknown. They fear the future. They fear to get their hands soiled. Hence, they remain where they are.

Life, history, literature are filled with stories of people who remain forever standing at the door, not daring to cross the threshold. Samuel Beckett's play, *Waiting for Godot*, comes to mind. The play ends with these words: "Well, shall we go? Yes, let's go. They do not move."

The longest journey begins with a single step. When Jacob stepped from his mother's tent to that of his father it was the first step of the longest journey of his life.

Do you remember a time when you made a fateful step that led you to an unexpected place?

Jacob keeping Laban's flock. *Gustave Dore*

7.

ENCOUNTERING THE ETERNAL THOU

Presence is not what is evanescent and passes but what
confronts us, waiting and enduring.

Genesis
Vayetze
28.1-32:3

JACOB LEFT BEER-SHEVA and ran northwards in the direction of Haran, to his mother's birthplace, Paddan Aram. As he ran he kept looking back over his shoulder to see if Esau was following him. When he was sure he had cleared a distance between himself and his brother, he sat on a rock, wiped the sweat from his face and neck and thought to himself, what have I brought on myself! Here I am, a fugitive, without protection, without food, with only the clothes on my back, on my way to a foreign land, without a map to guide me. What good to me now is the blessing I wrestled from my father? His reverie was short lived for he noted the place of the sun in the sky. He had to get out of the desert before darkness settled in.

Jacob's first Encounter with God

He walked quickly. In a few hours the sun would set. With quick steps, almost in a run, he went forward. But suddenly he was stopped. No matter how he tried, he could not go forward. Something invisible, like a huge wall, blocked his path. The more he tried to go forward, the more irresistible became the wall. And worse still the sun was playing tricks on him. Its last rim was sinking behind the horizon. It should not set for another three hours. Before he could think another thought heavy shadows of darkness crept upon him and enclosed him. Stupefied, he surrendered to the moment, gathered the stones lying about his feet, made a pillow of them and lay down. In sheer exhaustion he fell into a deep sleep. Or was it sleep! He was in an unfamiliar world. A ladder planted on the earth reached up to an opening in the heavens. All the angels of the surrounding land were ascending. Colliding with them, new angels were descending to earth.

Jacob wasn't alone. He felt a Presence. Then he heard a voice. He listened. The Voice said, "I am YHWH." Jacob's mind took a somersault. He had studied Torah during the long hours he sat in his mother's tent. He came to know about YHWH, how YHWH had created the world and even spoken to his grandfather, Abraham. He thought he would like to hear YHWH speak to him but not now that he had been so deceitful. The Voice continued, "I am the God of Abraham, and the God of your father, Isaac."

At those words Jacob remembered the promise God had made to his grandfather, Abraham, and his father, Isaac—the land on which he was sleeping belonged to the family and here he was fleeing from it. The Voice continued, "I will give this land to you and your descendants." Jacob thought to himself, but I am leaving it, never to return.

As if reading his mind, the Voice said, "Your descendants will be as numerous as the grains of dust on the earth; they will populate this land, north and south, east and west, and the whole earth will be blessed because of you and your progeny."

Jacob was now trembling. He had just robbed his brother, told lies to his father, and had with him a blessing that was not his. How could this be? Does the Voice not know what I have done? Then the Voice said, "Here, I am with you. I will watch over you wherever you go and I will bring you back to this soil." Oh, You do know, thought Jacob, You have not abandoned me. The Voice replied, "Indeed, I will not leave you."

Jacob awoke from his dream world. He was lying on the ground. Everything was the same as the night before, yet everything was different. The several stones he had placed together for a pillow had all joined together into one stone! He was no longer afraid. He no longer felt isolated. The world was suddenly a friendly place to be. Where was his fear and guilt of the night before? Gone! And in their place, a profound peace and joy filled his being. Bowing his head, Jacob exclaimed, "YHWH is in this place and I did not know it. This is none other than a house of God and that is the gate of heaven." He took the large stone, a combination of all the stones he had arranged for his pillow, and set it up. He poured oil on it and said, "Here is the house of God."

His feet, which were no longer heavy and weighed down with guilt, lifted him up and carried him forward on his journey.

Jacob's second Encounter with God[45]

Jacob was surprised by the extent of his new energy. He traversed the long distance from Canaan to Haran, his mother's country, with a lightness of heart and foot previously unknown to him. When he arrived in Haran he stopped at a well where there were three flocks of sheep and some shepherds. The shepherds were waiting for the other flocks to arrive before they lifted the heavy stone from the well's mouth. Jacob approached them and asked, "Do you know Laban, the son of Nahor?" "Yes," they replied, "Here comes his daughter Rachel."

Jacob looked up and saw Rachel coming with her flock of sheep. As she approached, he saw that she was graceful and beautiful. He felt powerfully drawn towards her. Embarrassed by his feelings, he ran to the well, heaved the heavy rock from the mouth of the well and watered Rachel's sheep. "How did he do it?" the shepherds asked one another. Though he had opened the well before its proper time, no one dared challenge him. When Jacob finished watering her sheep he stopped before Rachel who had been watching him the whole time. With tears streaming down his cheeks, he kissed her. He looked tenderly into her eyes. She smiled at him. He said, "Your father's sister, Rebekah, is my mother." "She is!" Rachel fairly screamed in delight. She turned and ran to tell her father, Laban, the exciting news.

When Laban saw Jacob, his first thoughts were of all the gifts he had received from Eliezer, Abraham's servant, who had gone looking for a wife for Isaac. Here was Isaac's son and the son of his sister. Looking at Jacob he said, "You are my bone and flesh. Stay with me. I have work for you. Tell me what will be your wages." Jacob replied, "I will serve you seven years for your younger daughter Rachel." Now Laban had two daughters, Leah, the older and Rachel. Though it was not the custom to marry off the younger daughter first, Laban agreed to Jacob's proposal.

The seven years passed quickly and the day for the wedding was fixed according to plan. Laban gathered all the people together and made a great

---

45 Genesis 29:14 –32:1

drinking feast. The next morning when Jacob awoke he discovered that not Rachel but Leah was beside him. Jacob turned to Laban and said, "What have you done to me. Was it not for Rachel that I served you? Why have you deceived me?" Laban replied, "Such is not done in our place, giving away the younger before the firstborn; just fill out the bridal-week for this one, then we shall give you that one also, for the service which you will serve me for yet another seven years."

The rogue! Deceiver! Jacob thought. No sooner had he said those words than he remembered how he had deceived his father and stolen Esau's blessing. Was he being given an opportunity to repair for his sins, "measure for measure"! After the week was up he married Rachel in a quiet wedding and worked another seven years for her.

During this time, Jacob prospered in wealth and in progeny. Through Leah he had six sons and a daughter and two more sons through her maidservant, Zilpah.[46] Leah often wept at nights for she knew that Jacob didn't love her. Even though her contacts with him were cold, she willingly went in to him for she hoped that if she had children by him, he would love her. She named her first born son, Reuben, meaning *looked*: "Because the Lord has *looked* on my affliction; surely now my husband will love me." She bore a second son and called him Simeon, meaning *heard*: "Because the Lord has *heard* that I am hated." She had a third son and she named him, Levi, meaning *joined*: "Now this time my husband will be *joined* to me." Then she had a fourth son and she named him, Judah, meaning, praise: "This time I will praise the Lord."

In the meantime, Rachel, the beloved wife, was barren. She too suffered, not from lack of love, but from a sense of divine neglect. She did everything she could to become pregnant. One day Reuben, Leah's son, came in from the field with an armful of mandrakes, plants that were slightly narcotic and were known to have aphrodisiacal virtues. Desperate, Rachel said to Leah, "Please give me some of your son's mandrakes." Leah said to her, "Is it a small matter that you have taken away my husband? Would you take away my son's mandrakes also?" Rachel said, "Then he may lie with you tonight for your son's mandrakes." Rachel did become pregnant shortly after that and she had a son whom she called Joseph. Jacob refused to believe that it had anything to do with the mandrakes. It was God who remembered Rachel and opened her womb.

---

46 An ancient custom allowed a wife to give her maidservant to her husband in order to have children by her whom she would call her own.

After Rachel bore Joseph, and was pregnant with Benjamin, Jacob over-heard Laban's sons saying, "See how rich Jacob has become at our expense. He has taken all that was our father's. From what was our father's he has made all this weighty-wealth." Jacob also noticed that Laban's countenance had changed towards him. He knew he had to do something or he would be killed. His grandfather had told him to watch out for such moments of discomfort for it was in such a moment that his grandfather heard the words, "*Lech Lecha*, go forth, to the land that I will show you." Then Jacob heard a Voice, "Return to the land of your ancestors, to your kindred! I will be with you!"

He called Rachel and Leah to the field where his flock was grazing and told them what God said to him. Rachel and Leah responded in chorus, "Is there any portion or inheritance left to us in our father's house? Does he not regard us as foreigners? For he has sold us, and he has been using up the money given for us. All the property that God has taken away from our father belongs to us and to our children; now then, do whatever God has said to you."

So together with their children and all their possessions they fled with-out telling Laban. Ten days later Laban heard of their escape and pursued them.

There is no Impression without Expression

1. "But suddenly he was stopped. No matter how he tried, he could not go forward. Something invisible, like a huge wall, blocked his path. The more he tried to go forward, the more irresistible became the wall."

The wall is some difficulty that prevents you from going forward.

What is the wall in your life? What have you done to go around the wall, go through the wall, under the wall or over the wall? Once you are stopped by a wall, the only option you may have left is to transcend it, which is spiritual growth. When a grain of sand gets stuck in an oyster shell the oyster turns it into a pearl. A diamond is coal under pressure for a long time. And roses grow in manure!

How do you transcend a wall that you can't remove?

2. While the word Wall can be a name for God, the name Place is an actual

name that is given to God. The word for Place in Hebrew is *HaMakom*. "He came to The Place and stayed there for the night," means that he came to God, *HaMakom*, and stayed with God for the night.

a) "Jacob came to a certain place" (Genesis 28.11). A more literal translation from the Hebrew is, "Jacob encountered the place." The Hebrew word, *paga*, means to encounter someone or something that forces one to stop. He encountered God. God stopped him in his tracks.

b) "Now he took one of the stones of the place." Not "one" of the stones but "of" the stones: "Now he took of the stones" (Rashi's translation) lying about his feet and made for himself a pillow. While he was sleeping, these stones became one, " So Jacob rose early in the morning, and he took *the* stone that he had put under his head and set it up for a pillar and poured oil on the top of it. The melting of the stones into one stone symbolizes the unifying process that was taking place within Jacob's own fragmented self and the healing of past memories.

c) "He had to spend the night there, because the sun had set." The Hebrew suggests that the sun dropped beneath the horizon before its time so that darkness descended, leaving Jacob no choice but to stay there for the night (Rashi on Genesis 28.11). Why would God cause the sun to set prematurely? God wanted a meeting with Jacob. In the Midrash Rabbah, it is written:

> This teaches that the Holy One, blessed be God, caused the sun to set prematurely, in order to speak in privacy with our father, Jacob. This may be compared to a king's close friend who visited him occasionally, and the king would then order, "Extinguish the lamps, for I desire to speak with my friend in privacy." In the same way God caused the sun to set prematurely so that he might speak to our father Jacob in privacy.

Suggestion: Choose a comfortable place to sit and relax. Take a few deep breaths. Allow the tension to leave your body. Imagine a place where you would like to be or recall a place you would like to revisit. Perhaps by the sea, on a mountaintop, or deep in the forest. Note the quality of light...the temperature and feel of the breeze....the smell of the flowers. Relax. Let your worries seep out of you as you listen to the sounds. You may sense a presence within you or you may sense that the place has a presence. Let the power of the moment fill you. Smile.

3. A wall separated Jacob and Leah. Yet the wall did not hide Leah from God but rather made her more visible: When the Lord *saw* that Leah was unloved, he opened her womb (Genesis 29.31). Her fourth son, Judah, became the ancestor of the Jewish people and from him the Jews derive their name. From him, too, descends the Messiah. Is it not ironic that all this happens through Leah, the unloved wife!

Can you identify with Leah? Can you envision yourself transcending a wall if you can't break it down or get around it?

Jacob and Esau. *Gustave Dore*

8.

I Have Seen Your Face

In the relationships through which we live,
the innate You is realized in the You we encounter

HAVING EMBRACED LABAN, his father-in-law, in a gesture of peace, Jacob set off to continue his journey home. Suddenly, such a crowd of angels surrounded the camp that Jacob exclaimed, "*Mahanaim*, this is God's camp!"[47]

Genesis
Vayishlah
32:4- 36:43

The joy and excitement of the moment were short-lived. Jacob was at the border of his homeland and the face of his brother Esau confronted him. He had some mending to do there. To begin with, he sent messengers to him with this message, "I have lived with Laban as an alien, and stayed until now; and I have sent to tell my lord, in order that I may find favor in your sight." He chose that word 'lord' with intent.

The messengers returned and said, "We came to your brother Esau, and he is coming to meet you, with four hundred men."

Terror suddenly seized Jacob's heart. His face turned pale and his feet began to feel like jelly. Falling prostrate on the ground, he pleaded, "O God of my father Abraham and God of my father Isaac, O YAH, You who said to me, 'Return to your country and to your kindred, and I will do you good,' I am not worthy of all your steadfast love and faithfulness that you have shown me. Deliver me, please, from the hand of my brother, from the hand of Esau, for I

---

47   Genesis 32.2

am afraid of him; he may come and kill us all, the mothers with the children. Yet you have said, 'I will surely do you good, and make your offspring as the sand of the sea, which cannot be counted because of their number.'"

When he said that prayer he felt better. He knew his next step. It must be generous, actually overwhelming. From his flocks and herds he chose two hundred female goats and twenty male goats, two hundred ewes and twenty rams, thirty milch camels and their colts, forty cows and ten bulls, twenty female donkeys and ten male donkeys. He then sent them with servants, in relays. Each time that Esau asked to whom do these belong, the servants must answer, "They belong to your servant Jacob; they are a present sent to my lord Esau; and moreover he is behind us."

Jacob thought to himself, no matter how badly I have treated my brother, surely gifts like these will wipe the anger from his face and when I see him he will lift a kindly eye to me. Nevertheless, Jacob decided to be cautious. He took his two wives, his two maids, his eleven children and everything he had and sent them across the Jabbok stream. He himself stayed behind for the night.

When everyone was out of sight, Jacob walked back and forth until darkness settled in. He lay down on some dead weeds against a bolder for the night. But sleep evaded him. The trickling of the water of the Jabbok River and the night sounds didn't calm his restless soul. Finally towards midnight he thought he had dozed off to sleep when just as suddenly he was startled by a sound of someone walking. He reached out his hand to protect himself. A mysterious stranger grabbed him. Jacob struggled with him. All night long they struggled until dawn began to appear. With the dawn the night visitor became nervous. Trembling, he struck Jacob on the hip and knocked it out of its socket and then straining to get away, he screamed, "Let me go, for the day is breaking." Jacob put a vice grip around him and said, "I will not let you go, unless you bless me." The stranger hesitated, "What is your name?" Jacob answered, "Jacob." The stranger said, "You shall no longer be called Jacob, but Israel, for you have struggled with God and with humans, and you have won." Then with an energetic yank, he broke from Jacob's grip, went a distance, turned towards Jacob, blessed him and disappeared. He dissolved from sight as mist from the sun.

Jacob stood there looking, peering into space, hoping to see someone. But no one was there. Baffled, he asked himself if he had a bad dream. He tried to move but as soon as he took a step he groaned in pain. He grabbed unto a rock to steady himself. He moved this way and that until he heard something crack, a bone slip back in place. He tried standing. That was better. Yet he limped. No, it wasn't a dream. He had met someone.

The water was still trickling down a path in the gulley. Hawks swept over the ravine in large overarching circles. A light breeze caressed Jacob's forehead. He stood there. Again he heard the words, "Your name shall be Israel."

"Israel! Israel!" he repeated. What does Israel mean? he wondered. He broke the name into syllables, *Is-ra-el.* Suddenly he understood. *Is-ra-el, one-who-sees-God.* Yes, I've seen God!

Jacob was trembling with a new kind of excitement. He repeated the names over and over. Israel! Jacob! Israel. When he noticed that the sun was high in the sky and its hot beams were pouring down on his head he bent down once more to see if he could steady himself. He could. He picked up a boulder at his feet and planted it on the spot of the night struggle. In a loud voice, he said, "Your name is *Peniel,* face of God, for truly I have seen God face to face, and yet my life is preserved."

He quickened his step. He was anxious now to be reunited with his family and to meet his brother.

Esau! He is my brother. He doesn't feel heavy any more, he thought. Lifting up his eyes, he saw Esau coming towards him with four hundred men. Fear grabbed at him. Quickly he divided the people and the animals into two camps. If Esau struck one camp, the other would be left to escape.

Jacob, now Israel, went to the front of the line. Every few feet, as he drew closer to Esau, he prostrated on the ground before him. Seven times he did this in accordance with common court ritual of bowing seven times as one approaches a monarch. On his seventh prostration, Esau who had been observing him, parted from his warriors and walked towards Jacob. When Jacob stood up, they were face to face with each other. Jacob saw not animosity but kindness in the eyes of Esau. Esau saw a new Jacob standing before him. Esau stretched out his arms to Jacob. Jacob did likewise. Suddenly they were locked in one another's embrace. When they loosened their grip of each other, Esau fell upon Jacob's neck and kissed him.

During this time, Leah and Rachel, their maids and all the children had drawn near and were looking on. When Esau looked up and saw the women and children, who now bowed before him, he said, "Who are these with you?" Jacob replied, "The children who God has graciously given to your servant."

Jacob's use of the word "servant" was not lost on Esau. Looking at the smiling faces of all those gathered around him, Esau continued, "What do you mean by all this company here?" Jacob answered, "To find favour with my lord." This time Jacob used the word, "lord!"

As Jacob pressed gifts on his brother, Esau said, "I have enough, my brother; keep what you have for yourself."

Brushing away a tear that fell when he heard Esau call him, 'my brother,' Jacob said, "No, please; if I find favour with you, accept my presents from my hands, for truly to see your face is to see the face of God."

What an extraordinary statement for Jacob to make, "to see your face is to see the face of God." Both Leah and Rachel heard his words and smiled. They couldn't help it. They hugged each other. The little kids saw their mothers embracing and they too embraced each other. The camels nudged at each other's lips. The goats began bleating and the little goats went catapulting around with sounds of *meee meee*. Even the angels seemed to have gathered for this momentous encounter for Leah said to Rachel, "I hear a breeze in the air like the sound of angels' wings." Rachel too felt her heart warmed and looking up at Leah said, "You are my sister, whom I love."

Jacob's voice rose above theirs and they heard him say to Esau, "Please accept my gifts that I've brought to you, because God has dealt graciously with me, and because I have everything I want." So he urged him, and Esau took them. Then Esau said, "Let us journey on our way, and I will go alongside you." But Jacob said to him, "My lord knows that the children are frail and that the flocks and herds, which are nursing, are a care to me; and if they are overdriven for one day, all the flocks will die. Let my lord pass on ahead of his servant, and I will lead on slowly, according to the pace of the cattle that are before me and according to the pace of the children, until I come to my lord in Seir."

So the brothers parted in peace. Esau returned home and Jacob journeyed westwards to Succoth and onwards to Shechem.

After a tragic sojourn in Shechem, Jacob travelled with his family and flocks to the place where God had revealed the divine self to him when he first fled from his brother. He had come the full circle of "there and back again." He called the place *El-bethel*, House of God (Gen. 35.37).

There is no Impression without Expression

Buber wrote, "The lines of relationship intersect in the eternal Thou. Every single Thou is a glimpse of that."

Since the quality of my relationship to God is tied to my relationships to others, the time I spend on improving these relationships is a divine task. My main concern in this divine task is to straighten out my relationships with others, and look kindly upon all. How others perceive me is not my task.

Isaiah said, "In the wilderness prepare the way of the Lord, make straight in the desert a highway for our God."[48] In the wilderness of broken relationships, sow healing. Where there is hatred, love; where there is discord, harmony; where there are shadows, light.

John the Baptist repeated these words, "Make straight the way of the Lord."[49] And Jesus said, "Leave your gift there before the altar and go; first be reconciled to your brother or sister, and then come and offer your gift."[50]

The story is told of a heroine who said to the hero, "When we cross this enormous mountain we will be at our destination." The hero replied, "This enormous mountain is our destination."

Who is blocking your road to God? What person? What relationship? How do you remove the block or change the "It" to a "Thou?" Paradoxically, when you say "I" with your whole being the block can become a Thou.

---

48 Isaiah 40.3
49 John 1.23
50 Matthew 5.24

Joseph is sold. *Gustave Dore*

9.

THE BELOVED OF HIS FATHER

The stature of a person depends on the strength of the I in the basic word I-Thou. The way one says I decides where a person belongs. The severed I is dissonant. But how beautiful is the I in relation, the I in conversation.

Genesis
Vayeshev
37:1-40:23

ALL ABANDON JOSEPH. His brothers hate him. They strip him of his clothes and his dignity. They throw him into a deep pit invested with scorpions and snakes. Then they drag him out and sell him to merchants who bring him down to Egypt. In Egypt he is falsely accused, stripped of his royal robes and flung into an Egyptian dungeon. Yet these events are the fire that honed Joseph into a *zaddik*, a righteous person, the only personality in the Hebrew Scriptures to which this epithet has been applied. What is the glue that held Joseph's personality together and prevented it from being shattered into a thousand pieces? The secret lies in his response to his Thou.

Joseph is Stripped of his Garment

Joseph was the son of Jacob 's favorite wife, Rachel, as well as the son born to Jacob in his old age. Joseph's brothers hated him because he was the favorite of his father. They particularly disliked the multi-colored coat his father gave him as a mark of preference. Joseph innocently baited their hatred by bringing ill reports of them to their father and in his naiveté shared with them his fantastic dreams of superiority. He was the standing grain sheaf in the field to whom all the other brothers bowed. He was the royal personage to whom the sun and the moon and eleven stars did homage. His brothers not only hated him; they were jealous of him.

One day when his brothers were tending their sheep in Shechem, Jacob foolishly called Joseph to him and said, "Come, pray, look into the well-being of your brothers and into the well-being of the sheep, and bring me back word." Joseph left immediately. He found them in Dothan. When they saw Joseph approaching, they said to one another, "Here comes the master dreamer! So now, come, let us kill him and throw him into one of these pits and say: An ill-tempered beast has devoured him!" But Reuben said to them, "Do not shed blood! Throw him into this pit that is in the wilderness, but do not lay a hand upon him!"

So when Joseph came to his brothers, they tore from him his ornamented coat, the mark of his identity as the favoured son of their father. Stripped and naked with but a few underclothes on him, they mocked him, "Now we will see what will become of his dreams." Grabbing him by the head and feet they threw him into a pit.

Joseph landed on stony ground and noted that it was empty, empty of water. But it was empty only of water. Creeping things were moving all about. Looking more closely into the darkness, he saw that the pit was infested with snakes and scorpions.[51] The blood left his face and he changed from a ruddy complexion to a pale white paste, and from white he turned green.[52] He became frozen to the spot until he heard a voice. It was the voice of a dove cooing. It was speaking to him with the voice of a young woman: "Even though you sit in the darkest dungeon, fear no evil, for I am with you." Joseph looked about to see where the voice was coming from. But all he saw as he peered into the darkness were dozens of eyes staring at him. Before him was a large scorpion with eight legs and a pair of pincers. The last segment of its tail was bulb-like. Joseph knew that it had a stinger that contained poison glands. Cracked words came out of Joseph's throat as he looked into its eyes, "What are you doing here?" Joseph said. The scorpion answered, "What are you doing here? This is my home. But don't worry. I won't hurt you. I'm not nearly as dangerous as humans think I am." Joseph moved away from it but as he did so, a snake with a smooth dry texture and belly scales crawled over his leg and arm.

In the meantime the brothers had gone off to eat their noonday meal. As they were eating, a caravan of Ishmaelites approached on its route to Egypt.

---

51 Rashi Genesis 37:24. "Why then does the verse say 'no water was in it?'" It says this to imply that there was no water in it but there were snakes and scorpions in it."

52 Ibid., *Midrash Tanhuma*, Parashat *Vayyigash*, on "Come let us sell him to the Ishmaelite."

Judah said, "Let's not kill our brother but rather sell him to the Ishmaelites. So they hauled Joseph out of the pit and sold Joseph to the Ishmaelites for twenty pieces-of-silver, the price of ten pairs of shoes at 2 silver pieces each.[53] The Ishmaelites sold him to the Midianites, and the Midianites sold him into Egypt.[54] The brothers noted how Joseph had aged. He was an old wizened man with grey hair and a distant look.

Joseph left his Garment in her Hands

Potiphar, a courtier of Pharaoh and a prominent Egyptian, bought Joseph from the Midianities and set him to work. Potiphar came to like Joseph. He saw that everything that Joseph did he did well so he made him overseer and put him in charge of all that he had. Potiphar's wife also liked Joseph. In a short time Joseph regained his handsome form and beauty of appearance. Potiphar's wife could not resist him. When she looked on him, she desired him. But Joseph said to her, "My master has put me in control of everything in his estate and has withheld nothing from me except you, his wife. So how could I do this to him? I would be sinning against God." But Potiphar's wife would not take No for an answer. One day when he came into the house and no one was around, she grabbed him and said, "Lie with me." Joseph broke away and left his garment in her hands.

He wished he had held unto his garment. The loss of his garment stirred up memories of another time when he was stripped of his clothes. He tried to recall that moment but all he could remember was the nakedness he felt, as though someone had removed his identity from him. Something similar was happening now. He would lose face with his master and courtiers.

He heard her call the servants of the house and accuse him of rape. When her husband appeared she cried out, "The Hebrew slave whom you brought into this house tried to rape me. When I cried out, he left his garment in my hands and fled."

Potiphar's anger flared up at his wife's words. He took Joseph and threw him into the dungeon prison with the other prisoners of the king. Dressed in prison clothes and treated like a non-person with no rights to a trial or any form of justice, Joseph found it easy to identify with the other prisoners in the jail.

---

53 *Midrash Tanhuma*, Parashat *Vayyigash*, on "Come let us sell him to the Ishmaelites."
54 Rashi 30:28, "The sons of Jacob pulled Joseph from the pit, and sold him to the Ishmaelites, and the Ishmaelites sold him to the Midianites, and the Midianites sold him to Egypt."

Joseph now a Prisoner in Egypt

The chief jailor took an immediate liking to Joseph. He put him in charge of all the prisoners. One day Joseph was awakened by a dove cooing. He recognized her for she was speaking to him in the voice of a young woman, "Go to cell number fifty." Joseph rose quickly and went to cell number fifty and found two men sitting silent and dejected. He said to them, "Why are your faces in such ill-humour today?" Now one of these men was Pharaoh's chief cupbearer and the other his chief baker. Both of them had displeased Pharaoh and he had them cast into prison. Both of them had dreamt disturbing dreams during the night. In chorus, they replied, "We have dreamed dreams, and there is no interpreter for it!"

Joseph said to them, "Are not interpretations from God? Pray recount them to me!"

So the chief cupbearer told his dream to Joseph, and said to him, "In my dream there was a vine before me, and on the vine there were three branches. As soon as it budded, its blossoms came out and the clusters ripened into grapes. Pharaoh's cup was in my hand; and I took the grapes and pressed them into Pharaoh's cup, and placed the cup in Pharaoh's hand." Then Joseph said to him, "This is its interpretation: the three branches are three days; within three days Pharaoh will lift up your head and restore you to your office; and you shall place Pharaoh's cup in his hand, just as you used to do when you were his cupbearer. But remember me when it is well with you; please do me the kindness and make mention of me to Pharaoh, and so get me out of this place. For in fact I have done nothing that I should have been put into this dungeon."

The cupbearer was happy and he swore that he would not forget Joseph.

When the chief baker saw that the interpretation was favourable, he said to Joseph, "I also had a dream: there were three cake baskets on my head, and in the uppermost basket there were all sorts of baked food for Pharaoh, but the birds were eating it out of the basket on my head."

Joseph hesitated. Should he tell him what he saw? The Voice said, "You must tell him. If he knows what the future holds for him, he can choose his response." So Joseph answered him and said, "This is its interpretation: the three baskets are three days; within three days Pharaoh will lift up your head—from you—and hang you on a pole; and the birds will eat the flesh from you." Joseph paused and looked at him. He wondered if the baker would return to Pharaoh or escape the moment he got out of prison.

Three days later, Pharaoh had a birthday. He put on a feast for all his servants. The cupbearer and the chief baker were released and it happened to them as Joseph had predicted it would happen. The cupbearer was restored to his former glory and the chief baker was hanged. But no sooner was the cupbearer restored to his former glory than he forgot Joseph and the promise he had made to him.

Meanwhile, Joseph lingered on in prison. He tried to recall his past, the past he had before he was brought to Potiphar's household but it was clouded in mist. He knew from Potiphar's accusation that he was a Hebrew. "A Hebrew slave!" she derisively called him. Sometimes he had nightmares when he felt insects crawling over his body and serpents twining around him. At other times his dreams were filled with light. He walked through golden fields of harvested grain where stooks of barley stood in rows, with the straight, blonde tresses of their heads streaming down to the ground. He liked the feel of their silken hair as he rearranged the stooks in the form of subjects before their king. Often when he awoke he smelled not the stale stench of the prison latrines but the scent of cut grass, of jasmine, and mint and blueberry and clover. His heart fairly smiled when he heard "his" dove cooing outside the window of his prison cell. She told him that his days in prison were numbered.

The day came for his release. The jailor called him. "Joseph, Joseph, Pharaoh wants to see you. Shave. Here is a change of clothes. Pharaoh has dreams that no one can interpret and someone told him that you interpret dreams." Joseph replied, "It's not me who interprets dreams. God does. But I'm glad to get out of here."

There is no Impression without Expression

Suffering! Joseph held no bitterness towards those who caused him to suffer. He refused to ask why he suffered? He knew that to ask the *why* of suffering was to go down the wrong road, while to search for ways to respond to suffering led to life.

Suffering! There once lived a rabbi by the name of Levi Yitzhak who prayed this prayer to God: "How could I bear to ask why everything happens as it does. I do not beg You to reveal to me the secret of your ways—I could not bear it. But show me one thing; show it to me more clearly and more deeply; show me what this, which is happening at this very moment means to me, what it demands of me, what You, Ruler of the world, are telling me by way of it."

Suffering! The poet Rumi wrote,
>Whatever comes, comes from a need,
>a sore distress, a hurting want.
>
>Mary's pain made the baby Jesus.
>Her womb opened its lips
>And spoke the Word.

Suffering! Jesus suffered not to free us from suffering but to show us how to suffer.

Suffering! Since the path to God is paved with suffering can you describe your own path to God? When suffering loses its value, healing is instantaneous. When we realize the true purpose of suffering it is no longer suffering. Now ask yourself, "What am I suffering for? What am I getting out of suffering?"

Joseph before Pharaoh. *Gustave Dore*

10.

GULF OF SEPARATION

The present exists only insofar as encounter and relation exist.

Genesis
Miketz
41:1- 44:17

JOSEPH WAS A man without a past. His family, his life in Canaan, were little more than a blur in his consciousness. The shock of the pit not only turned his hair white but wiped out his memory of family and country.

Joseph remained in prison for two more years after the release of Pharaoh's chief baker and cupbearer. Then Pharaoh had two dreams that no one could interpret. Pharaoh dreamed that he was standing by the Nile and seven sleek fat cows came up out of the water and grazed in the reed grass. Then seven other cows, ugly and thin, came up out of the Nile after them, and ate up the seven fat cows. Pharaoh awoke and fell back asleep and dreamed again. This time he saw seven plump ears of grain growing on one stalk. Then seven thin blighted ears of grain came and swallowed up the seven full ears. None of his magicians could interpret his dreams for him. The chief cupbearer hearing of this, remembered Joseph who had interpreted his dream, and ran to tell Pharaoh about him.

Pharaoh sent for Joseph. Joseph was hurriedly brought out of the pit, shaved and clothed in new clothes. Pharaoh looked at him and said, "I have had a dream, and there is no one who can interpret it. I have heard it said of you that when you hear a dream you can interpret it." Joseph answered Pharaoh, "It is not I; God will give Pharaoh a favorable answer." After Pharaoh told Joseph his two dreams, Joseph said, "Pharaoh's dreams are one and the same; God has revealed to Pharaoh what he is about to do. There will be seven years of plenty throughout the land of Egypt followed by seven years of famine that will consume the land. Therefore let Pharaoh choose a wise and discerning person who will save enough during the years of plenty to provide for the years of famine.

Pharaoh was pleased with this proposal. He said, "Can we find anyone else like this—one in whom is the spirit of God?" Pharaoh said to Joseph, "Since God has shown you all this, there is no one so discerning and wise as you. You shall be over all the land of Egypt, over my house, and all my people, only with regard to the throne will I be greater than you." Removing his signet ring from his hand, Pharaoh put it on Joseph's hand; he arrayed him in garments of fine linen, and put a gold chain around his neck. Pharaoh gave Joseph the name Zaphenath-paneah and he gave him Asenath daughter of Potiphera, priest of On, as his wife. Joseph was thirty years old when all this happened.

For seven years the land produced abundantly. In every city Joseph stored the grain, which was now piled up beyond measure, from the fields around it. He worked hard and was known throughout the land. He and Asenath had two sons. When the first son was born, Joseph said to Asenath, "Let's name him *Manasseh* (causing to forget) because God has caused me to forget all my hardships and all my family. Asenath agreed because she knew that he was suffering from amnesia and could remember nothing of his past before his arrival in Egypt. When they had their second son, Joseph said, "Let's call him, *Ephraim* (double fruitfulness), because of all the fruitfulness God caused to come upon us in the land of my affliction. Asenath agreed to that name also for she knew that God had abundantly blessed them.

After the seven years of plentiful harvest, the seven years of famine began. It spread throughout Egypt and all the countries around. Only in Egypt was there food. When the surrounding countries heard of this they came to Egypt to buy grain. Jacob did likewise. He sent ten of his sons down to Egypt to buy grain. He kept his youngest son, Benjamin, the son of Rachel and the full brother of Joseph at home.

The Wall has a Crack
Joseph Weeps for the First Time

When the brothers entered the presence of Joseph they bowed low to the ground. Joseph was startled. A faint memory returned. Did he have brothers? As he gazed at them, prostrate before him, he saw a glimmer of bent sheaves, bowing before an upright sheaf. Startled and filled with anguish, he spoke harshly, "Where do you come from?" "From the land of Canaan," they replied. "You are spies! You have come to spy out the land." "No, no," they replied. "We have come to buy food. Our father, who is old, sent us. We are his sons. We, your servants, were twelve brothers, the youngest is now at home and the other is no more."

Joseph stood still, shocked by what he heard. The fog in his head seemed to be clearing. Could these be his brothers? He must find out. He would send them home with food but keep one of them as hostage until they returned with the youngest son, of whom they spoke. When the brothers learned of this, they began speaking among themselves in Hebrew, not suspecting that Joseph could understand them. They said to one another, "Truly we are guilty: concerning our brother!—that we saw his heart's distress when he implored us, and we did not listen. Therefore this distress has come upon us!" Joseph caught his breath. Tears began to flow. He quickly turned away so they would not see him crying. Then he returned to them and had Simeon bound before their eyes. He then gave orders that their bags be filled with grain, that they be given provisions for the journey home and the money they had paid for the grain be put into their bags.

The Walls Begin to Crumble
Joseph Weeps a Second Time

Although Jacob swore to his sons that his youngest son would never go into Egypt, he was forced to relent because of the famine. Earlier, Reuben had tried to convince the father to let Benjamin go with them. But Jacob absolutely refused. Then Judah, his third eldest son, said to him, "Let Benjamin go with me so that we will live and not die of starvation. I pledge my life for his life." Hungry, with no food in the house, Jacob said, "Go if you must, but take some gifts of the land as a present, some choice fruits in your bags, a little balm and a little honey, gum, resin, pistachio nuts, and almonds. And that money that you found in your sacks bring it back. And may God Almighty grant you mercy before the man, so that he may send back your other brother and Benjamin. As for me, I am bereaved of my children."

The brothers returned to Egypt and stood before Joseph. When Joseph saw Benjamin, he didn't know what to do to express his joy so he ordered a great feast to be prepared. The brothers were mystified and terrified. They went to the steward of Joseph's house to return the silver they had found in their sacks. But the steward said that he had already received the money in payment, "It is well with you, do not be afraid! Your God, the God of your father, placed a treasure in your packs for you—(for) your silver has come in to me."

Then the steward took Simeon, their brother, out of prison and brought him to them. Together they went into Joseph's house. Seeing Joseph, they gave him their gifts and bowed down before him. Joseph went to them and asked about their welfare. Unable to restrain himself, he asked, "Is your old father well, of whom you spoke? Is he alive" Then seeing Benjamin, his full brother, his mother Rachel's son, he asked, "Is this your youngest brother of whom you spoke to me?" The question broke open a door within him. Sobs welled up inside him. He rushed to the chamber next door and wept and wept. When he got control of himself, he washed his face, came out and ordered the meal to be served.

The Walls Collapse
Joseph Weeps Uncontrollably

When the banquet was over, Joseph commanded the steward of his house to fill the men's sacks with food, as much as they could carry and to put each man's silver in the mouth of his sack. As for Joseph's goblet, he was to put that in the "mouth of the youngest son's pack" The men went off at the light of daybreak. They were just outside the city when Joseph's steward caught up with them, according to Joseph's commands, and accused them of stealing, "Is not this (goblet) the one that my lord drinks with? And he also divines, yes, divines with it! You have wrought ill in what you have done"!

The brothers denied the accusation and foolishly said, "He with whom it is found among your servants, he shall die, and we also will become my lord's servants!"

When the brothers' sacks were searched, the goblet was found in Benjamin's sack. They returned to Joseph's house and flung themselves down before him to the ground. Judah said, "What can we say to my lord?   God has found out your servants' crime! Here we are, all of us, servants to my lord."

Joseph replied, "Heaven forbid! Only the man in whose hand the goblet was found—he shall become my servant, but you—go up in peace to your father."

Judah stared at Joseph thinking, "This man is like a deep pit sealed tight." Holding his eye, he strode towards him. When he was face to face with him he began to speak. The words tumbled out of his mouth faster and faster until they became a torrent that formed a rope that reached down and burst open the stopped-up well inside Joseph.

Joseph caught his chest and began to weep. Blusteringly he ordered all the attendants to leave. When the last attendant had left, Joseph broke out into loud sobbing. The Egyptians in the fields heard the sound. Pharaoh heard it. The brothers stood in shocked silence. Finally, Joseph looked at them and between his sobs he said, "I am Joseph. Is my father still alive? Yes, I, I am Joseph your brother, whom you sold into Egypt. But do not be upset that you sold me, for it was not you that sent me here, but God. It was to save life that God sent me on before you. Please, come close to me." Stretching forth his arms Joseph hugged each of his brothers, weeping as he did so. His brothers wept in turn.

After the brothers left, Joseph sat alone for a long time. His "I" had stretched. It was no longer bounded by Egypt and Pharaoh's court. Jacob was his father. Rachel was his mother. These were his brothers. He had a sister, too. Her name was Dinah. Wiping away his tears, he repeated to himself. "I am Joseph your brother. Yes, I am Joseph your brother. "

There is no Impression without Expression

1 Many people refuse to cry. Many people cannot cry. It was difficult for Joseph to cry. The first time he cried he simply, "turned away from them and wept." The second time, "his feelings were so kindled toward his brother that he had to weep." The third time, when "he put forth his voice in weeping, the Egyptians heard, Pharaoh's household heard." Tears can unlock the dungeons within.

When is the last time you cried? What happened?

2.The journey back to the self is a journey from I-It relationships to I-Thou. After a long journey of meeting strangers along the road, Joseph can say to his own brothers, "Come closer."[55]

Draw a horizontal line. At one end write birth and at the other end write death. Destiny is not death; destiny is the journey. You are not going towards death like a clock running down but you are walking towards your destiny. All your previous life is merely prologue. Prologue has two meanings, the *first word* and towards *meaning*.

Where are you on the line? Where are you going?

---

55   Genesis 45.4

Joseph reveals himself. *Gustave Dore*

11.

RELATION IS RECIPROCITY

Love is responsibility of an I for a Thou

Genesis
Vayigash
44.18-47.27

JUDAH LET GO of his brother Joseph's embrace; the tears were still coursing down both of their cheeks. When he promised his father, Jacob, that he would stand surety for Benjamin and bring him safely back to his father, he never dreamt that he would return not only with Benjamin but with the news that Joseph was alive and regent of all of Egypt.

Yes, he, too, had hated Joseph. It was at his suggestion that Joseph had been sold to the Ishmaelites and he, together with his brothers, took Joseph's robe, dipped in goat's blood, to their father Jacob deceiving him into believing that a wild animal had devoured Joseph. How often after his own anguished cries over the death of his sons had he heard again the tortured cry of his father, who at the sight of Joseph's robe cried out, "It's my son's robe. A wild animal had devoured him; Joseph is without doubt torn to pieces." He remembered even unto this moment how Jacob tore his garments, put on sackcloth, and mourned day after day for his son. None of them could comfort him. What would his father say when he said, "Father, your son, Joseph is alive and well and wants to see you."

Judah retraced in his mind all that had happened in the last few hours. He remembered that he drew near to Joseph and stood face to face with him. He recalled the full feeling he had towards Joseph as though he were 'soul of my soul'. It was this feeling that gave him strength to stand his ground and look into Joseph's eyes and say, "O my lord, let your servant please speak a word in my lord's ears, and do not be angry with your servant; for you are like Pharaoh himself." Then he moved still closer to Joseph and spoke directly to him summarizing all the events that had taken place. He interspersed his words with, "You said," and "We said." He repeated the word "father" at least eleven times. The words he spoke were clearly written in his memory. He could recall his speech word for word:

> My lord asked his servants, saying, 'Have you a father or a brother?' And we said to my lord, 'We have a father, an old man, and a young brother, the child of his old age. His brother is dead; he alone is left of his mother's children, and his father loves him.'

> Then you said to your servants, 'Bring him down to me, so that I may set my eyes on him.' We said to my lord, 'The boy cannot leave his father, for if he should leave his father, his father would die.'

> Then you said to your servants, 'Unless your youngest brother comes down with you, you shall see my face no more.'

> When we went back to your servant my father we told him the words of my lord. And when our father said, 'Go again, buy us a little food,' we said, 'We cannot go down. Only if our youngest brother goes with us, will we go down; for we cannot see the man's face unless our youngest brother is with us.'

> Then your servant my father said to us, 'You know that my wife bore me two sons; one left me, and I said, Surely he has been torn to pieces; and I have never seen him since. If you take this one also from me, and harm comes to him, you will bring down my gray hairs in sorrow to Sheol.'

> Now therefore, when I come to your servant my father and the boy is not with us, then, as his life is bound up in the boy's life, when he sees that the boy is not with us, he will die; and your servants will bring down the gray hairs of your servant our father with sorrow to Sheol. For your servant became surety for the boy to my father, saying, 'If I do not bring him back to you, then I will bear the blame in the sight of my father all my life.'

> Now therefore, please let your servant remain as a slave to my lord in place of the boy; and let the boy go back with his broth-

ers. For how can I go back to my father if the boy is not with me? I fear to see the suffering that would come upon my father."

Judah also remembered that he held no bitterness towards his father when he repeated words like, "and his father loves him" and "my wife bore two to me." What I used to call the outrageous favoritism of our father for Joseph and Benjamin, the sons of Rachel, with no reference to our mother, Leah, used to rankle me to no end. But I had none of those feelings when I was speaking to Joseph. I truly wanted Benjamin returned to our father for I knew Father would die if anything happened to him. That is why I offered myself as a slave to replace Benjamin.

A great noise shook Judah from his reverie. The caravan of food and supplies arrived and the brothers were ready to depart for Canaan. He joined them and they set off. Joseph called after them and said, "Do not quarrel along the way." Judah smiled at those words. Previously, they might have irritated him, but they were as honey to him now.

Judah couldn't shake Joseph from his thoughts. For the first time in his life he felt that Joseph was truly his brother. He felt affection for him. He wanted to know more about what happened to him after they left him abandoned in the well. So deep was he sunk in his thoughts that he hadn't noticed that he was far behind the caravan. He could now faintly hear the steady rhythm of his brother's heavy boots treading the sands of the terrain up ahead. He quickened his steps and caught up to them. He walked beside the back camel allowing his own breath to mingle with the beast's heavy breathing. After long hours of walking and with night approaching, the brothers arrived at a clump of acacia trees in a wadi and decided to camp there for the night. They needed space not only for what they had brought with them but for what they were returning with. Pharaoh had given them ten he-donkeys and ten she-donkeys plus wagons and provisions not only for the journey back but also for the return journey with their father. By now they were hungry and looking forward to a good meal. Leah's sons, Simeon and Levi, Issachar and Zebulun, unhitched the animals and fed them, while Gad and Asher, the sons of Leah's maid, Zilpah, and Naphtali and Dan, the sons of Bilhah, Rachel's maid, prepared the meal. Benjamin was charged with making the coffee. Reuben and Judah went looking for enough wood and dried weeds to keep the campfire burning all night.

As they walked, Reuben took Judah's arm and said, "Hey, brother, that was a knock-out speech you made to Joseph. I never thought you were capable of such words as "Oh, my lord, let thy servant," and "My lord asked his servants." Several times you repeated "servant" and "lord." That doesn't sound like you? Then when you referred to our father you talked as if he had only one wife and two sons! Explain yourself." Judah said, "I was devastated when my two sons died. I began to understand our father's anguish at the loss of Joseph." "OK, OK," said Reuben, "but admitting wrong and offering all of us as slaves! It worked but how did you feel when you admitted that we were guilty?"

Judah then turned to Reuben. "How did you feel after you went into the tent of Bilhah and lay with her? Did you ever apologize to our father?" Reuben didn't reply. He simply lowered his eyes. Judah took his arm, "I did something worse than that. I lay with my daughter-in-law and got her pregnant."

"You did," said Reuben. "How did that happen?"

"My wife had been sick for a long time. Then she died. After my days of mourning were over I went up to Timnah to check on the sheep. I was feeling rotten. I was lonely and destitute. On the way, I saw a prostitute by the roadside. I said, "May I come in to you?" I offered to send her a goat from the flock. She asked that I leave a pledge of my seal and my staff as security. When my servant returned with the goat, he found no prostitute and was told that no prostitutes worked in that area. I wanted my staff and seal back but I didn't pursue it because I didn't want to become a laughing-stock. Some months later I was told that Tamar, my daughter-in-law was pregnant. I ordered her to be burned at the stake. As she was being brought to the pier, she sent my staff and seal to me with a note that said, "The owner of these is the father of my child." You can imagine how shocked I was. I didn't know that I had lain with my daughter-in-law. But I didn't want to be made a mockery of. She would soon be burned at the stake and the evidence gone up in flames. But something in me cried out, in words so loud that everyone around heard me, 'She is more in the right than I.' I took my pride in my hands and called off the death sentence."

"How was she more in the right than you?" demanded Reuben.

"Tamar was married to my oldest son, Er. He died. I told my son, Onan, to go into Tamar and raise up children for his deceased brother. He refused. Yes, he went in to her but he spilled his seed on the ground. He died because of his sin. So I said to my daughter-in-law, 'Remain a widow in your father's house until my son Shelah grows up.' So Tamar went to live in her father's house and waited for Shelah to grow up. Months passed, and years passed and Shelah grew up but I didn't arrange for the marriage. I was afraid that Shelah might die if he married her. So I procrastinated though I knew she needed to raise up issue to Er. When I read the note she sent on the way to her death, I saw my own fear and her bravery. She risked her life while I, the coward, sat back and did nothing. That's when I cried out, 'She is more in the right than I.'"

Reuben put his arm on Judah's shoulder. They sat together in silence. The clicking sounds of insects, like the tapping of fairy feet, intruded into the silence, as did the skirmishes of little animals scampering here and there in the light of the half moon. A light breeze left its coolness on their foreheads. They would have liked to stay longer but they knew they must move. As they rose to go, Reuben said, "Do you think some divine impulse made you say, 'She is more in the right than I?'" "I believe so," replied Judah, "but it is so much easier for me now to admit my mistakes. I used to think it was a sign of weakness; now I know it takes courage to admit wrong." Then he grasped Reuben's arm and said, "We must go. Our brothers will think we are lost."

All the brothers were asleep except for Benjamin. Benjamin, who was called a predatory wolf by his father and from whom descended Saul and Mordechai and Esther, was guarding the camp from night prowlers. When he saw the brothers, he ran forward to greet them, served them hot coffee with pita bread and herbs. After they had eaten, Judah and Reuben lay down beside each other and slept soundly until awakened by the excited voices of the brothers drinking coffee and the donkeys braying.

They were soon on their way. The closer they came to their father's house in Canaan, the quicker they traveled. When Jacob saw them coming from afar, he ran to meet them. The brothers cried out in chorus, "Joseph is still alive! He is ruler over all Egypt." Jacob straightened up. What did he hear! His son, Joseph, alive! Looking around he saw the wagons, the donkeys, and the provisions. He felt a new spirit coming back into him. He cried. He laughed. Finally he said, "Enough! My son Joseph is still alive. I must go and see him before I die."

There is no Impression without Expression

1.Reflect on Repentance (*teshuvah*) as "Love's responsibility of an I for a Thou."

    a. How does this differ from the definition of "Love is a feeling?" Who do you take responsibility for?

    b. The Judah who stands before Joseph in Egypt is not the same Judah who stood before Joseph in Canaan. How has he changed? Who does Judah love?

2. When Jesus said, "Just so, I tell you, there will be more joy in heaven over one sinner who repents than over ninety-nine righteous persons who need no repentance,"[56] he was not undermining the word "righteous" but rather giving it its true definition. "Perfectly righteous" describes a static position, which ends up in death. Repentance, which is a dynamic process, is the making of a righteous person because it makes our relationships right. Think of the last time you tried to mend a relationship. Would you describe what happened as an I-Thou encounter?

3. "Repentance is mightier than the sword"; "Great is repentance for it reaches to the Throne of Glory"[57]; "The place the penitent occupy the perfectly righteous are unable to occupy"[58].
If repentance is so powerful, why is it so difficult to repent? What does repentance require?
Can you recall a time when a serious situation was changed because of an act of repentance?

4. The name of Judah, *Yehudah*, in Hebrew, contains the four-lettered name of God, *YHWH*, which means, "God is here." What did Judah do to merit having the four lettered name of God embedded in his name? How did he make himself present?

5. Reconciliation is *making present*. Becoming present is forgetting the past and changing the context of the present. Changing the context of the present is to give birth to possibility.

Have you had an experience of reconciliation that has given birth to possibility?

4. Tamar took a big risk when she seduced her father-in-law in order to fulfill her destiny. Although what she did was perfectly legal in Hebrew law, she placed her fate in Judah's hands. Have you ever had the need to trust that someone else would do the right thing?

---

56   Luke 15:7
57   Yoma 68a
58   Ber. 34b

PART C

AND THEIR WORDS TO THE END OF THE WORLD

Jacob goes into Egypt. *Gustave Dore*

12.

ENCOUNTERING LIFE

*God's address to humans penetrates the events in all of our lives
and all the events in the world around us
and turns it into Torah*

Genesis
Vayehi
47:28-50:26

JACOB WAS NOW very old, one hundred forty-seven. He knew he was not old compared to his ancestors, yet he knew his days were numbered. Though he was lying in bed, sick and frail, and his eyes were poor, his mind was clear and alert. He had much to do before he died. He had sent for his sons and for Joseph's sons so that he could bless them before he died. He would ask them to promise to bring his body to Canaan and bury him in the cave of Machpelah, near Mamre, the land of Canaan, in the field that Abraham bought from Ephron the Hittite as a burial site. There Abraham and his wife Sarah were buried; there Isaac and his wife Rebekah were buried, and there also was buried Leah.

As he waited for Joseph to arrive, he recalled that it was seventeen years since he came to Egypt. How quickly the time had gone. What blessed years they were. He was living with his sons and their families in Goshen, the best part of Egypt, where Joseph according to Pharaoh's directives, had settled them. He said to himself, "I never expected such joy to come to me in these last years of my life. For twenty-two years I thought Joseph was dead and here he is, vice-regent of the whole of Egypt. I still feel the darkness of those years. How many times did I hold my son's coat, torn and bloodstained, in my arms? I watched those stains turn to yellow and then black. My son, my beloved son, torn-to-pieces by a wild beast! I refused any kind of comfort. It would be an insult to his memory. To those who offered me comfort, I said, 'No, I shall go down to Sheol to my son, mourning.' Thus I bewailed him. The heavy blanket of sorrow and depression that enveloped me got heavier, not lighter with the years. Then when I heard that he was alive, I refused to believe. How could it be possible! When I came into Pharaoh's presence and he asked me my age, I replied, 'The years of my earthly sojourn are one hundred thirty; few and hard have been the years of my life. They do not compare with the years of the life of my ancestors during their long sojourn.'

Yes, my spirit revived when I came to believe that Joseph was alive.[59] I quickly hurried to go down to Egypt. I remember leaving with my sons, their wives, their little ones, all our livestock and all that we had acquired in the land of Canaan. The wagons were full that Pharaoh had sent to carry our goods.

The nearer we drew to Beer-sheba, the more my depression lifted. I knew I had to stop there to offer sacrifice to the God of my father, Isaac. All agreed for they were tired. But I couldn't sleep. A terrible fear crept over me until my whole being shivered with terror. I turned and twisted. I thought my life would end. Then I heard a dove cooing. A Voice was calling me, "Jacob, Jacob." I remembered that Voice from long ago. I said, "Here I am." Then the Voice said, "I am God, the God of your father; do not be afraid to go down to Egypt, for I will make of you a great nation there. I myself will go down with you to Egypt, and I will also bring you up again; and Joseph's own hand shall close your eyes." I heard no more; I fell into a deep sleep. The morning awakened me. I didn't move. God had called me by name, my old name. Why? Because I hung on to my depression. Because I had not been living up to my new name of Israel. But God said, "Don't be afraid." No, don't be afraid, I repeated. God promised, "I myself will go down with you to Egypt." God will accompany me! In no time at all I was dressed and ready to continue the journey. I felt the same kind of lightness in my step that I felt when I set out for my mother's country after the night dream.

Jacob was shaken from his reverie when a servant entered and said, "Your son Joseph has arrived with his two sons, Ephraim and Manasseh.

---

59 Rambam, quoted in Avivah G. Zornberg, *The Beginning of Desire: Reflections on Genesis* (Philadelphia, 1995, p. 360). "Because of Jacob's sorrow and anxiety all the days of his mourning for Joseph, the holy spirit departed from him, until he was brought tidings that Joseph was alive: then, 'the spirit of Jacob revived'-which the Targum translates, 'The spirit of prophecy rested upon their father Jacob.' The Sages make the point in this way: 'Prophecy does not come to rest in the midst of lethargy, or of melancholy... but only in the midst of joy.'"

Joseph Enters With Ephraim And Manasseh

Though Joseph knew his father was a man of God he also knew that his father was subject to depression, which caused God's spirit to leave him. He hoped that today, above all days, that his father's spirit was full of joy for he wanted an abundance of blessings for his two sons, Manasseh and Ephraim.

When Jacob heard them approaching he collected his strength and sat up in bed. Ephraim and Manaseh were his favorite grandsons. He had often played with them. But when they entered he saw Joseph but not Ephraim and Manasseh. Instead he saw the descendants of these sons, the wicked kings of Jeroboam and Ahab from Ephraim, and Jehu and his sons from Manasseh.[60] The sight of future wickedness took the joy out of his soul. A heavy cloud of depression settled upon him.

Joseph saw the far distant look in his father's eyes. "Father!" he cried. Jacob was startled. He looked at Joseph and then at the two boys. "Whose sons are these?" he demanded. "These are my sons, whom God has given me," Joseph replied. Then taking his children out from between his knees he presented them to his father. Jacob reached out to the boys. As he embraced them a warm feeling came over him. Smiling, he turned to Joseph and blessed him:

> "The God before whom my ancestors Abraham and Isaac walked,
> the God who has been my shepherd all my life to this day,
> the angel who has redeemed me from all harm, bless the boys;
> and let them grow into a multitude on the earth."

Jacob then laid his hands on the heads of Ephraim and Manasseh and blessed them.
No sooner had he finished than there was a loud noise outside the door. Jacob's other sons had arrived.

Jacob and his Sons

A whole cohort of men poured into the room. Jacob quickly pulled his warm sheepskin over his shoulders and sat up erect in his bed. Gazing at them he felt overwhelmed and happy. These handsome twelve men were his sons. Lots of animal energy in them, he thought. My son, Judah, is a lion, Issachar

---

60   1 Kings 12:20ff.: 1 Kings 16:29ff; 2 Kings 10:30-31.

a donkey, Dan a serpent, Naftali a hind, Joseph an ox, Benjamin a wolf.

He broke off his musings and called (*yikra*) to them and said, "Gather around, that I may tell you what will call (*yikra*) to you in days to come." Jacob intentionally used the Hebrew word, *yikra*, for he knew it meant both to *call* and to *happen*. He wanted his sons to hear what could happen to them as a call to respond. He knew the story of Noah and how Noah could have prevented the flood. He also knew the story of his grandfather, Abraham. If only his grandfather had kept bargaining with God, Sodom and Gomorrah would not have been destroyed. He hoped his sons would come to know that life is not a series of preordained scripts but rather events that call for action.

In a strong voice he said, "Assemble and hear, O sons of Jacob; listen to Israel your father." Looking at Reuben he said, "Reuben, you are my first-born, my might and the first fruits of my vigor, excelling in rank and excelling in power. Unstable as water, you shall no longer excel because you went up onto your father's bed and defiled it." Turning to Simeon and Levi who had led the destruction of the inhabitants of Shechem because of their sister, Dinah, he said, "Cursed be their anger, for it is fierce, and their wrath, for it is cruel! I will divide them in Jacob, and scatter them in Israel." Jacob knew he had to say hard words to his sons. They referred to *Midat Hadin*, God's attribute of justice, which always accompanied God's attribute of mercy, *Midat HaRachamim*.

And so in turn, Jacob blessed all his sons. One could hear a pin drop so quiet had the room become. When they first entered, Jacob said, "Assemble and hear, O sons of Jacob; listen to Israel your father." He intentionally repeated that word "Hear" twice and he used both of his own names to let them know that he too had a checkered past.

When Jacob finished blessing his sons, his strength left him. He drew up his feet into the bed and breathed his last breath. For a moment the sons all stood in silence. A dove was gently cooing outside. A deep peace flooded the room.

Joseph threw himself on his father's face and wept over him and kissed him. And likewise the other sons wept over him and kissed him. Joseph then commanded the Egyptian physicians to embalm his father. It took forty days to do this. When the days of mourning were over, Joseph said to Pharaoh, "My father made me swear an oath that I would bury him in the land of Canaan where his ancestors were buried and where his wife Leah was buried."

Pharaoh answered him, "Go up and bury your father."

So Joseph and his brothers went to Canaan, with all the servants of Pharaoh, the elders of his household, and all the elders of the land of Egypt, as well as all the household of Joseph, his brothers, and his father's household. Only their children, their flocks, and their herds were left in the land of Goshen. Both chariots and charioteers went up with him. When they arrived in the land of Canaan they buried him there with his ancestors, as he had requested.

Joseph returned to Egypt with his brothers and all who had gone up with him.

Joseph's Brothers Are Afraid

On the return trip to Egypt the brothers spoke among themselves, "What if Joseph still bears a grudge against us and pays us back in full for all the wrong that we did to him?" They made up a story to tell Joseph. They approached him and said, "Your father gave this instruction before he died, 'Say to Joseph: I beg you, forgive the crime of your brothers and the wrong they did in harming you.' Now please forgive the crime of the servants of the God of your father."

Joseph turned to them, "Do not be afraid! Am I in the place of God? You have nothing to fear. Though you planned ill, God planned it for good so that many people would live. Do not be afraid. I will protect you and your little ones."

There is no Impression without Expression

1. We began this chapter with a quotation from Buber: "God's address to humans penetrates the events in all of our lives. And all the events in the world around us. And turns it into Torah."

These events are many and varied as springtimes and stars, waves and violins:

> Yes—the springtimes needed you. Often a star
> was waiting for you to notice it. A wave rolled toward you
> out of the distant past, or as you walked
> under an open window, a violin
> yielded itself to your hearing. All this was mission.

But could you accomplish it?[61]

God's address to you penetrates the events in your life like water seeping into soil. When was the last time you responded to a star waiting for you to notice it, a wave that rolled towards you out of the distant past, a violin that yielded itself to you?

2. God's address to you also penetrates the events of pain in your life. If you dialogue with a painful event in your life, you may have an I-Thou encounter with Pain. First, the pain needs to be named, that is, Cancer, Death of a friend, Lost Love. Then Cancer or Death needs to be addressed as a Thou. In addressing the object of pain as a Thou, you are encouraged to express the whole range of your feelings, from hate to love but don't stop with the negative feelings. Keep dialoging, which means that you will let the Pain talk back to you, until you have become friends with the enemy.

3. While you seek God in all people and all objects, you will want to guard against making any person or object into an idol no matter how holy you believe the person or the object to be. Examples abound of holy objects turned into idols or clichés. The cross, a symbol of unconditional love, was turned into a sword during the time of the crusades and enough pieces of the "true" cross were sold to build a forest. A story is told of a catholic policeman who rushed into a burning synagogue in New York City to save the Torah scrolls. Afterwards a rabbi, horrified at his imprudent act, exclaimed, "He risked his life, his wife and five children to save a piece of leather!"

What are the clichés in your life and what are the realities?

4. YHWH said, "I am YHWH." [62] YHWH stands beside you and says, "I am YHWH, your God. "Now you are to love YHWH your God with all your heart, with all your being, with all your substance!"[63] Has your involvement in these meditations made you a greater lover?

Presence is not what is evanescent and passes
but
what confronts us, waiting and enduring.

---

61   Rilke. *First Duino Elegy*
62   Genesis 28.13
63   Deut. 6.5

APPENDIX

AND I WILL BETROTH YOU TO MYSELF FOREVER

And I will Betroth You to Myself Forever[64]

You need God in order to be,
and God needs you—for that which is the meaning of your life.

Genesis
Bereshit
2.1-3

THUS THE HEAVENS *and the earth were finished, and all their multitude. And on the seventh day God finished the work that he had done, and he rested on the seventh day from all the work that he had done. So God blessed the seventh day and hallowed it, because on it God rested from all the work that he had done in creation.*[65]

When you read this passage from Genesis, does anything strike you as strange? Why not reread it again as though for the first time!

What about that line that says God rested on the seventh day from all the work that God had been doing? God rested! God ceased working! Are we to understand that God was tired from work and needed a rest? Could there be a deeper meaning than appears on the surface?

One way to deal with questions like this is to reread the preceding sentences to discover what is happening, who is speaking and who is being spoken to. For example, the passage on the seventh day and the double blessing bestowed upon it is preceded by a description of the creation of Adam and Eve and God's conversation with them. The two texts are connected through proximity.

The rabbis looked at the juxtaposition of the creation of the human person and that of the sabbath and they reasoned that it had only one meaning. The sabbath was the formal betrothal between God and the human person: "I will betroth you to myself forever."

---

64 Hosea 1.19
65 Genesis 2.1-3

Every sabbath thereafter would be a renewal and a deepening of the I-Thou relationship with God, with every human person and with the whole created universe. It would be a day set aside for lovemaking.

All we need do to gain a deeper understanding of the sabbath as God's day of making love to the human and the human making love to God is to look at some of the Jewish rituals surrounding the sabbath day. On the eve of the seventh day[66], before arriving in the synagogue, the Song of Songs is recited. The opening lines are:

> Kiss me, make me drunk with your kisses!
> Your sweet loving is better than wine...
> Take me by the hand, let us run together!
>
> My lover, my king, has brought me into his chambers
> We will laugh, you and I, and count
> Each kiss,
> Better than wine.[67]

Once in the synagogue, the cantor or the rabbi leads the congregation in love songs, one of the favorites being *Lechah Dodi*, "Come, my beloved, to meet the bride; the sabbath presence, let us welcome."

After the singing of the *Lechah Dodi*, the rabbi and the congregation pray several psalms from the Torah all leading up to the *Shema* and the *Amidah* prayer. The Shema proclaims, "Hear, O Israel: The Lord is our God, the Lord is one. You shall love the Lord your God with all your heart, and with all your soul, and with all your might."[68]

To love God with all one's heart, with all one's soul and with all one's might refers to an excessive love so powerful that one's being is totally involved in love of God, and constantly obsessed (*shoge*, mad) by it, as though ill with love sickness.[69] So the beloved cries out to the lover,

Kiss me, make me drunk with your kisses.
Your sweet loving is better than wine.

---

66 The day begins with the evening: "And there was evening and there was morning, the first day" (Genesis 1.5).
67 Songs of Songs, transl. by Ariel and Chana Bloch (Random House, 1995).
68 Deuteronomy 6.4-5
69 See chapter 3, above

After the synagogue service, family and guests return home. On the table are the two lighted candles that were lit at the time of sundown. Two loaves of challah, sabbath bread, made of two strings of dough intertwined with each other, are held aloft and blessed. These are all symbols of the I-Thou relationship between God and the individual, between God and the family, and between each of the members sitting at the table. The sabbath meal is a love feast, words of Torah are discussed, songs are sung, and people laugh and enjoy one another.

You Have Seen How I Bore You On Eagles' Wings

When God sent Moses to bring the Israelites out of Egypt, God said to him, "I will be with you; and this shall be the sign for you that it is I who sent you: when you have brought the people out of Egypt, you shall worship God on this mountain."[70]

Three months after the Israelites left Egypt they arrived at the mountain, which was Sinai. God called to Moses and said, "You have seen how I bore you on eagles' wings and brought you to myself. Now therefore, if you obey my voice and keep my covenant, you shall be my treasured possession."

Moses told the people what God had said and he told them to prepare to meet with God on the third day. The people all answered as one: "Everything that the Lord has spoken we will do."

When the third day arrived, God came in a dense cloud amidst thunder and lighting and said to all the people, "I am YAH your God, who brought you out of the land of Egypt, out of the house of slavery; you shall have no other gods before me." All of nature trembled at these words. The people stood in awe. God continued,

> Remember the sabbath day, to keep it holy. Six days you shall labor, and do all your work; but the seventh day is a sabbath to YAH your God; in it you shall not do any work, you, or your son, or your daughter, your manservant, or your maidservant, or your cattle, or the sojourner who is within your gates; for in six days YAH made heaven and earth, the sea, and all that is in them, and rested the seventh day; therefore YAH blessed the sabbath day and hallowed it.[71]

70   Exodus 3.12
71   Exodus 19-20

Moses had already given lessons in the desert to the people on the beauty of the sabbath and showed them how the sabbath demonstrated God's love for them, how it was an invitation to them to leave all their cares behind and enter into an I-Thou relationship with God, with one another, with the stranger in their midst and even with the animals. They would have no other care than the care for each other. They were to understand that when they entered into these relationships they were doing so in imitation of God in the creation story.

Keep My Sabbaths, For This Is A Sign Between Me And You

At a time when the Israelites were about to begin construction on the Tabernacle, a work of the greatest importance because the Tabernacle was to be a sign that God dwelt in their midst, God commanded them to stop working on its construction and keep the sabbath:

> And Yah said to Moses, say to the people of Israel, "You shall keep my sabbaths, for this is a sign between me and you throughout your generations, that you may know that I, YAH, sanctify you. You shall keep the sabbath, because it is holy for you; every one who profanes it shall be put to death; whoever does any work on it, that soul shall be cut off from among his people. Six days shall work be done, but the seventh day is a sabbath of solemn rest, holy to YAH; whoever does any work on the sabbath day shall be put to death. Therefore the people of Israel shall keep the sabbath, observing the sabbath through-out their generations, as a perpetual covenant. It is a sign for-ever between me and the people of Israel that in six days Yah made heaven and earth, and on the seventh day God rested, and was refreshed."[72]

Reread this passage and describe your feelings as you read it. Do you hear these words as words of love or threat?

The passage begins with, "I, Yah." Immediately your heart melts. Yah is God's name for mercy. "I, the merciful loving caring God." Then God says, "it is a sign between me and you." A sign of what? It is the wedding ring of the divine-human nuptials. Then God says, "You shall keep the sabbath for it is

---

72 Exodus 31.12-17

holy for you." Holy, because it is the time of your honeymoon with God.

Now if you have understood the first part of this text, you are ready for what follows: "Every one who profanes it shall be put to death." God doesn't put us to death. The community doesn't put us to death. We choose death. Remember Buber's words at the beginning of this chapter: You need God in order to be, and God needs you—for that which is the meaning of your life. Away from God, we die.

Jesus Went To The Synagogue, As His Custom Was, On The Sabbath Day

And he came to Nazareth, where he had been brought up; and he went to the synagogue, as his custom was, on the sabbath day.[73]

Again he entered the synagogue, and a man was there who had a withered hand. They watched him to see whether he would cure him on the sabbath, so that they might accuse him. And he said to the man who had the withered hand, "Come forward." Then he said to them, "Is it lawful to do good or to do harm on the sabbath, to save life or to kill?" But they were silent. He looked around at them with anger; he was grieved at their hardness of heart and said to the man, "Stretch out your hand." He stretched it out, and his hand was restored. The Pharisees went out and immediately conspired with the Herodians against him, how to destroy him.[74]

These texts from the New Testament about Jesus and the sabbath are interesting from different aspects. First we note Jesus' observance of the sabbath. He went to the synagogue, *as was his custom.* There he prayed the prayers of the synagogue of his time: "Hear, O Israel: The Lord is our God, the Lord is one. You shall love the Lord your God with all your heart, and with all your soul, and with all your might." When he entered the synagogue he saw a man with a withered hand. He said to him, "Come forward." Then he said, "Stretch out your hand." Love is responsibility of an I for a Thou.

But the tone of the text is not so much one of love but of conflict. Why? What is happening? To answer this question you need to know something

---

73   Luke 4.16
74   Mark 3.1-6

about the history of the text. An historical examination of the text shows that Jesus himself was a Pharisee. According to Pharisaic principles, Jesus did not break the sabbath. "To do harm" and "to kill," were always unlawful, not only on the sabbath. Healing was also permitted on the sabbath. The Pharisees declared that it was permissible to treat someone with laryngitis even if it entailed work: "If a man has a pain in his throat they may drop medicine into his mouth on the sabbath, since there is doubt whether life is in danger, and whenever there is doubt whether life is in danger this overrides the sabbath."[75]

In the light of what has been said, how can we explain this line, "The Pharisees went out and immediately conspired with the Herodians against him, how to destroy him." The only plausible explanation is that this reflects not the time in which Jesus lived, but the tension that existed between the followers of Jesus and the Jewish community at the time when Mark wrote the gospel, which was several years after the death of Jesus.[76]

The sabbath for Jesus as well as for the Jewish community to which he belonged was a treasured gift from God. It was the sign and renewal of the covenant.

No Impression Without Expression

1. The first honeymoon in history took place between God and the human person on the first sabbath: "I will betroth you to myself forever." What happened on that first sabbath is repeated on every sabbath since then. Ask yourself, "How does God make love to me? How do I make love to God?"

2. "The seventh day is a sabbath to YAH your God; in it you shall not do any work."

The day reserved for the divine self is obviously a day also for you, for your family, your staff and even your animals. But only you can give your day to God as only you can give yourself to God. The Hebrew text is addressed to you, in the singular not in the plural: "You shall remember the sabbath day and make it holy."

---

75 M Yoma 8.16
76 '85 *Notes on Nostra Aetate*: The Gospels are the outcome of long and complicated editorial work. The authors of the four Gospels selected some things from the many that had been handed on by word of mouth or in writing, reduced some of them to a synthesis, and explicated some things in view of the situation of their Churches.

From what you know of the sabbath day, what can you do to live in the spirit of sabbath?

The spirit of sabbath is expressed in I-Thou relationships. On sabbath you will want to make a special effort to live in an I-Thou relationship with members of your family, your friends, and your neighbors. It is a time when you will try to forget the hurts of the week and look kindly upon everyone and everything. The sabbath is a day of meetings, meeting with God, meeting with others, and meeting with yourself, not with an agenda, but simply to be present. Every I-Thou relationship is an I-Thou relationship with your eternal Thou.

3. "Remember the sabbath day, to keep it holy. Six days you shall labor, and do all your work; but the seventh day is a sabbath to YAH your God."

You have probably heard talk of God's transcendence and God's immanence. Those words express how we experience God in our I-It and our I-Thou relationships.

I-It relationships, which are necessary, predominate in work and are relationships that exist for a purpose, that is, "in order to." A doctor examining a patient to discover the cause of the pain is in an I-It relationship. At the same time, the doctor may be having an I-Thou relationship, which is what is happening when a doctor relates to the person rather than just the pathology. I-It relationships have an agenda. I-Thou relationships have no agenda and no expectations.

When you are involved in I-It relationships, God often appears to be distant and transcendent. When you are in an I-Thou relationship, God is experienced as immanent, present. Letting go of work, even for a pause, is an easy entrance into the present.

The sabbath day is a day of presence. God is there to meet with you but are you there to meet with God? Will you stop work? What preparations will you make for the day? How will you make love to God?

The custom of lighting sabbath candles is one way you can enter into the intimacy of the day. First, light two sabbath candles. Then cover your eyes with your fingers and say a blessing over the light. Open your eyes again and behold the light casting its glow round you, a sign that you have stepped into sacred time.

3. What should be your attitude if you have to work on the sabbath? Try to foster I-Thou relationships with all whom you meet. In other words, try to see the person with whom you are working not as a means to an end but as a person.

Do you have to work this coming sabbath? How can you make it an I-Thou day?

4. You will know that you are keeping the sabbath if you find delight in it. Delight isn't something that comes uninvited. You need to do something in which to delight. It is customary to gather together as a family or with friends to have a special meal with discussion on a topic from the Torah portion of the week. In addition to this one spends quality time with family and friends. Visiting an elderly aunt, going with children to the swimming pool, can all be part of the delight of the sabbath.

Name a sabbath activity that is not for the purpose of distraction but one that enables you to be more present.

6. The following page gives you a format to use for entrance into the sabbath if you are new to the sabbath and want to get started.

7. Sabbath observance is also for Christians because God gave the seventh day to the whole of humanity at creation. Sunday, the first day of the week, is the day Christians commemorate the resurrection of Jesus. Sabbath observance adds to the celebration of Sunday as it adds to its uniqueness.[77]

8. The caption for this chapter reads: *You need God in order to be, and God needs you—for that which is the meaning of your life.*

You need God for the very meaning of your life, but most exciting of all, God needs you for the uniqueness that is you. How do you react when you are told that God acually needs you?

---

77 Fritz, M, *Sabbath Rest and Sunday Worship: We are entitled to both.* www.batkol.info

A Sabbath Evening Table Celebration

(The table is set with a white tablecloth, flowers and two candles)

1. Gathering Hymn [*or another hymn of your choice*]:
   Holy God, we praise Your Name, Lord of all, we bow before You.
   All on earth Your scepter claim, All in Heaven above adore You.
   Infinite Your vast domain, Everlasting is Your Name.

   Hark the loud celestial hymn; Angels' choirs above are rising.
   Cherubim and Seraphim, in unceasing chorus praising.
   Fill the Heaven's with sweet accord, *Holy, Holy, Holy YAH!*

2. One participant reads:
   Thus the heavens and the earth were finished, and all their multitude.
   And on the seventh day God finished the work that he had done,
   and he rested on the seventh day from all the work that he had done.
   So God blessed the seventh day and hallowed it, because on it
   God rested from all the work that he had done in creation (Gen. 2:
   1-3; Fox).

3. Look at the two sabbath candles, which are lit eighteen minutes before
sunset every Friday night. Let the glow of the light reflect on your hands.
Then draw the light to your face.

4. All of the participants read:
   The week has ended. The Sabbath with its peace has come. Together let
   us pause and allow its meaning to enlarge our lives: Be praised, O YAH,
   our God, who has blessed us with the gift of Sabbath. Bless us, YHWH,
   with Sabbath joy, with Sabbath holiness, and with Sabbath peace.

5. Blessing on those present. The Host may do the blessing over the
gathered assembly or each person can bless at least one of the table
companions.

6. Blessing of the wine:

בָּרוּךְ אַתָּה יְיָ אֱלֹהֵינוּ מֶלֶךְ הָעוֹלָם

Barukh atah Adonai, Eloheinu, melekh ha-olam
Blessed are you, Lord, our God, sovereign of the universe

בּוֹרֵא פְּרִי הַגָּפֶן (אָמֵן)

borei p'ri hagafen (Amein)
Who creates the fruit of the vine (Amen)

7. Blessing of the bread (if there is a Jewish bakery in your neighborhood, you will be able to buy a special sabbath bread called *challah*):

בָּרוּךְ אַתָּה יְיָ אֱלֹהֵינוּ מֶלֶךְ הָעוֹלָם

Barukh atah Adonai, Eloheinu, melekh ha-olam
Blessed are You, Lord, our God, King of the Universe

הַמּוֹצִיא לֶחֶם מִן הָאָרֶץ (אָמֵן)

hamotzi lechem min ha'aretz. (Amein).
who brings forth bread from the earth. (Amen)

8. All then enjoy the Sabbath dinner.

9. Between the main meal and the dessert, the Host introduces the Sabbath Table Talk based on the Word of God.

10. Sabbath Table Talk concludes with some Hebrew or other songs.

11. Dessert, accompanied by more table songs.

12. Conclusion: The Magnificat, to the tune for Amazing Grace.
    [*Another song may be substituted if you wish.*]

My soul proclaims the LORD my God: my spirit sings Yah's praise!
Yah looks on me and lifts me up, and gladness fills my days.
All nations now will share my joy; Yah's gifts have been outpoured.
This humble one Yah has made great. I magnify the LORD.
For those who love Yah's holy Name, Yah's mercy will not die.
Whose strong right arm puts down the proud, and lifts the lowly high.
Yah fills the hungry with good things, and sends the rich away.
The promise to Ab'ram and Sarah is filled to endless day.
Most holy and creating LORD, to You be thanks and praise,
To you be glory, power, and might, from age to endless age!

Final blessing:

May YHWH *bless you and keep you. May the divine countenance shine upon you and be gracious unto you. May* YHWH *grant you peace.* (Num. 6:24-26)
　　In Hebrew:

Yevarek-khah Adonai ve-yish-ma-re-khah
Ya-er Adonai panav ele-khah vee-hu-nekhah.
Yissah Adonai panav ele-khah
ve-ya-sem lekhah shalom.

יְבָרֶכְךָ יְהֹוָה וְיִשְׁמְרֶךָ׃

יָאֵר יְהֹוָה פָּנָיו אֵלֶיךָ וִיחֻנֶּךָּ׃

יִשָּׂא יְהֹוָה פָּנָיו אֵלֶיךָ

וְיָשֵׂם לְךָ שָׁלוֹם׃

ISBN 142513709-1

9 781425 137090